'Finding a
one who v
. . . in this l
– **John Gill**

MW01592464

'A brilliant book that everyone interested in moving over stone should read! At first it sounds like a difficult read, with concepts detached from actually doing it, but Francis Sanzaro manages to describe complex ideas without ever losing touch to the challenge and joy of bouldering - highly recommended!' – **Udo Neumann**, filmmaker and author of *The Art and Science of Bouldering*

'. . . today, you rarely see much literature and reflection coming out of anyone. That just changed. Francis Sanzaro stopped what he was doing and took the time to reflect on bouldering and what it means to him and why he does it. The result is his impressive new book *The Boulder: A Philosophy for Bouldering*. In it, he presents some of the most thoughtful and interesting writing I've ever read about this sport.' – **Andrew Bisharat**

'The language we use to describe climbing is pretty rudimentary, relying on lots of waving of the arms. If climbing is to become a serious competitive sport – and it seems to be heading that way – then there will be major advances in this area . . . this book will confirm what we know already: that there is a lot more to bouldering than meets the eye.' – **Dave Flanagan**, author of *Bouldering Essentials: The Complete Guide to Bouldering*

Francis Sanzaro is an international climber and Editor-in-Chief of *Gym Climber* and *Ascent* magazines. He holds a PhD in Philosophy of Religion and is the author of *The Infantile Grotesque: Pathology, Sexuality and a Theory of Religion* and *Society Elsewhere: Why the Gravest Threat to Humanity Will Come From Within*. His writing has appeared in *The New York Times*, *The Scotsman*, *The Huffington Post*, *Adventure Journal*, *Outside*, *The Baltimore Post Examiner*, and *Continental Philosophy Review*. He now lives, climbs, and writes in Carbondale, amongst the mountains of Colorado.

STONE COUNTRY EDITIONS

Francis Sanzaro

⌘

THE BOULDER

A Philosophy for Bouldering

⌘

The Boulder: A Philosophy for Bouldering, 2nd edition

Copyright © Francis Sanzaro, 2021

First edition published 2013 by Stone Country Press Ltd.
Second edition published 2021 by Stone Country Press Ltd.

The right of Francis Sanzaro to be identified as the author
of this work has been asserted in accordance with the
Copyright, Designs and Patents Act, 1988.

A CIP catalogue record for this book is available from the British Library.

Designed by Stone Country

Printed and bound by Severn Print

ISBN 978-0-992887-65-0

www.stonecountrypress.co.uk

CONTENTS

FOREWORD by JOHN GILL	7
PREFACE TO THE SECOND EDITION	11
ACKNOWLEDGEMENTS	13
NO STYLE NEEDED	16
THE ART OF MOVEMENT	19
THE ATHLETIC BODY	24
THE BOULDERING BODY	27
THE STAGE	33
FIELDS, CLOCKS, COACHES	38
GILL	42
FLASH, RAMPAGE, FUTURE	45
VISIONS OF EXCESS	50
GRACE AND TRUTH	56
TECHNOLOGIES V. TECHNOLOGY	59
WHERE DOES A BODY BEGIN?	65
SPORT OF TOUCH	69
ARCHITECTURE	72
MOVEMENT I	79
MOVEMENT II	86
ENTROPY	90
IMPROV	96
ORGANIZED DESPAIR	100
SEEING THE FIELD	108
OUVRIR, OR OPENING A PROBLEM	116
ABSTRACTION: ATHLETIC SURFACES	129
MYSTICISM AND ATHLETICS	136
THE BOUT	142
LIPS AND FINGERS	149
A GENERATIVE MACHINE	152
FURTHER READING	161

FOREWORD
– JOHN GILL –

Does bouldering exist as a form of pure or artistic athletics, safely removed from cultural pressures? I wager it does not. It is very unlikely that any activity, especially if it involves large numbers of participants, can persist in a sort of societal vacuum, its goals and practices formulated by an elite who dine at some distant table well away from the larger community. Although I thought of myself as individualistic and imaginative back in the early and mid-1950s when I first bouldered – and I suppose I was with respect to the existing American climbing community – I did not comprehend the effect the larger culture had upon my 'innovations'. I formulated my efforts in a context I made no attempt to understand. What I did seemed 'natural'.

Gymnastics had come upon the world stage, largely through the spectacular performances of Soviet athletes via the miracle of television, and I had just taken a college course in the sport – so I saw climbing on small rocks as a gymnastic enterprise, assuming it fundamental that form is as important as difficulty. And the enormous loss of life during World War Two and, later, the Korean War had the general effect of dampening the spirit of risk when it seemed optional. A generation of young men had been decimated. Those who returned and became civilian rock climbers had been schooled by the US Army to practise three-point suspension and value safety above all else. Accordingly, I suppressed the notion of jeopardy in bouldering, using a top rope on problems where a fall might result in severe injuries. Three-point suspension was another matter.

It is true that, in the late 1950s and early 1960s, I became for a time obsessed with the bizarre notion of what might many years later be called free-solo exploration. With as much precision as possible, I was finding my limits as a rock climber – what lines I would neither cross nor attempt. This seemed to be the ultimate endgame of climbing, virtually unheard of in America and lying far beyond incremental extensions of the sport. Many years later, John Bachar would elevate free soloing to an art, but at the time the culture's attitude towards risky adventure was only gradually changing as the baby boomers neared young adulthood, and the horrors of the 1940s became more distant. Science and engineering were flourishing, and men were steeling themselves for the challenges of space exploration. Nevertheless, my conviction that bouldering should be relatively safe persisted, and I found it ironic that my 1961 ascent of the 30ft (9m) Thimble – definitely a climb for me, not what I considered a bouldering problem – was seen by some as the first step towards highball bouldering.

Yvon Chouinard informed me in 1957 that what I was doing was called 'bouldering'. I naively assumed the California climbers had coined the word while practice climbing at places like Stoney Point. During the early 1960s, Rich Goldstone told me of Fontainebleau's 'boulder climbers', and I recall being a bit disconcerted at the thought that others might have beaten me to the punch.

Many years later, after I had stopped bouldering and had retired as a mathematics professor, I had the leisure and inclination to research the origins of the sport. I was delighted to discover that the British had used the word 'bouldering' as early as the late 19th century and had imparted to bouldering its aura of serious but light-hearted fun. These studies placed in perspective my contributions to the sport.

My predecessors included Oscar Eckenstein, a British engineer who was among the pioneers of rock climbing as a sport and who had, in 1892, conducted a bouldering competition among natives in the Karakorum, giving the winners one rupee each. Eckenstein discovered modern balance climbing on his eponymous boulder in Wales in the 1890s, instructing leading climbers of the time, including Geoffrey Winthrop Young and J. M. Archer Thomson, in the technique. Pierre Allain, the great French climber and equipment designer, wrote of the possibility of treating boulder climbing seriously in Fontainebleau's forests in *Alpinisme et Compétition*, published in 1947. His group of 'Bleausards' wore rock-climbing shoes designed by Allain and stepped off small rugs onto the rock. All that remained for me to do – although I was not aware of it at the time – was introduce gymnastic chalk and controlled dynamics into bouldering (and rock climbing), and encourage the acceptance, in the larger climbing community, of bouldering as a legitimate pursuit, to be practised wherever boulders were found. Thus, 'modern bouldering' began, prefaced by the skilful and ingenious accomplishments of several international generations of devotees.

And now we find ourselves in yet another cultural milieu where risk, once a vice, is now a virtue. Highballers are admired, and the top-rope is rarely seen, replaced by flimsy mats giving the illusion of safety from four body lengths above the ground. As in modern gymnastics, where once form was exceedingly important, most contemporary bouldering focuses almost entirely on difficulty, an illusory and ill-defined measure dependent on a host of physical attributes. Gymnastic judges treasure extreme difficulty so highly they are reluctant to deduct points for lack of form – whereas half a century ago gymnasts were required to do compulsory routines, simple exercises where form and grace were paramount. In another athletic realm, can you remember the last time you saw a figure skater doing figure-of-eights in a competition? However, the changes to gymnastics and skating were not entirely due to an intentional shift in the importance of form. Rather, they arose to relieve boredom and create more excitement for spectators, especially those in the television audience. Bouldering is no exception: the soaring dynamics, the gasping and the screaming as bodies part from the rock makes formal competitions – in an age of extreme sports – at least modestly attractive to the general public.

That is not to say there are no other interpretations of bouldering, but finding a climber who perceives bouldering as a moving meditation, or one who values form and style far beyond difficulty, is a daunting task. The 'governing bodies' of the sport are riveted to alphanumerical scales that, in essence, convey the tendencies of routes and problems to spit off competitors. It is far simpler to rank boulderers by their highest numerical accomplishments than by the more nebulous assessment of form and style.

Into this maelstrom of athletic overindulgence, Francis Sanzaro, a climber and philosopher, brings a soothing and penetrating analysis. Not merely of the technical aspects of the sport, but of its philosophical and aesthetic underpinnings and its ties to the cultures in which it grew – a notable task since many enthusiasts place bouldering alongside skateboarding and other seemingly 'juvenile' antics. If bouldering – whose progenitors were professional men living in the Victorian and Edwardian ages – has any hope of surviving as a serious adult sport, it needs its own analytical literature. In this book, Francis Sanzaro takes a significant step in that direction.

John Gill

⌘

PREFACE TO THE SECOND EDITION
– FRANCIS SANZARO –

Bouldering was my first love. I was a gymnast when I first discovered climbing, and so at an intuitive level, I understood the level of exertion needed to make hard moves, the timing required, the mastery. It just made sense.

Early on, I grew fond of highballs, compression moves and hard mantels. Thanks to gymnastics, I understood finicky movement because that is what bouldering is all about. It's not about grades and ego and impressing people and all that, well, it is for some, but for the majority, it is there, in existence as a sport, because people have fallen in love with it. That love leads one to try to master its moves, and in this mastery, there is something singular. I do many other types of climbing – trad, ice, sport, alpine – but the chalk on my hands during those early years I reserved for bouldering.

After high school, I chose the college I would attend because it was in proximity to Horsetooth Reservoir, the stomping grounds of John Gill. It was the only college I was accepted to, and I got in under academic probation. If I didn't get a B average, I had to go home. That was motivation enough. For the first time in my life, I stayed and got an A on my report card. My parents were so shocked they thought I had forged it.

I had read an article by the late Craig Leubben about the legendary Gill and his early bouldering at Horsetooth, a beautiful collection of Dakota sandstone blocks with a long season, grand vistas and classic problems. It is just west of Fort Collins, Colorado. Gill was the godfather of bouldering. An amateur gymnast, he was the first to introduce chalk to our sport, had a more muscular physique than 99% of top climbers today, and climbed V9 (Font 7c) in the 1950s in shit climbing shoes, at a time when most of the climbing world thought 5.10 was hard. To say he was visionary is an understatement. I wanted to follow in his footsteps, go where he went, climb what he did. Doing Gill's problems today is, for me, reliving history. I'm honoured for him to write the Foreword to this book. He remains an inspiration, and we all owe him a lot.

Like any devotee, I've scrubbed countless moss-covered boulders looking for new lines, spent hundreds of hours driving around and hiking for new boulders, and pored over Google Maps scanning for promising areas. Most of the time, I'd find choss, but when it did work out, and you'd turn a corner to find a giant block sitting there, just waiting for you – there's nothing better. I think this is all I did for a decade straight, well, that and attend grad school, which, it turns out, provides an excellent schedule for a climber.

It appears the print run of the first edition has sold out, and so John Watson, owner and editor of Stone Country Press, wanted to do a new and updated edition. A great idea. The result is this revised second edition of *The Boulder*, and I went through the original book line by line, updating the ideas, trends, research and issues. It is a better book now, in my estimation.

The future will gaze upon boulder problems as relics of an ancient era and ask questions like: *What could they have seen in them? What was it they were really doing? How could climbing a boulder represent an outstanding achievement?* What follows here is a series of reflections intending to answer those questions and perhaps give a language to bouldering – to what we are performing in the woods, mountains or gyms.

My philosophy does not claim to be comprehensive. There is no unifying thread other than *the task* – investigating bouldering movement. In this sense, I am in accord with Bruce Lee's ideas about having no style (or form) in this investigation, for as it goes with ideas, so it goes with bouldering – one must employ any tactic to achieve the goal. Or, to cite avant-garde American filmmaker John Waters: 'Technique is nothing more than failed style.' One must not get caught in the trap that there is only one way of doing things or one sequence to send – one must think across boundaries and create new concepts where there is no existing word or phrase to utilise. You know, try new things.

Francis Sanzaro, 2021

ACKNOWLEDGEMENTS

A book is always a team effort, and John Watson, my editor, deserves much credit for bringing this book into its final shape. He's a brilliant thinker, writer, editor, and, most important, climber. Since it was an earlier text of his – *Stone Play: The Art of Bouldering* – that first caught my attention as a philosophical and artistic exploration of bouldering, without his shared vision and passion for bouldering, this book would not have been possible. The fact that we are now onto the second edition is a good sign. I am personally indebted to John Gill for his instinct since he had seen promise in this book when I sent him what can hardly be termed a 'first draft'. Moreover, Gill's early essays from the 1960s ought to be talking points for any serious engagement with bouldering, as it was during this time when the sport was still young, naive and vulnerable. In other words, it was by reading how Gill conceived the sport *then* that influenced how I thought about it *today*.

Initially prompted by a good friend and professor Ed Mooney of Syracuse University, I began to combine my philosophical and theoretical interests with my background in athletics, especially climbing. I started jotting down ideas – connecting bouldering movement to dance theory, gymnastics, philosophy, art, architecture, football, track and field – and before I knew it, the text had grown considerably. Most importantly, I read some early Gill essays and was greatly influenced by his vision of the sport. After that, I began to see bouldering differently – as a sport of our era, as an outgrowth from our time, and as a contemporary form of expression with many parallels in our culture. For those reasons, bouldering must be discussed alongside other cultural and intellectual currents, for it is within this matrix that we get a glimpse of what it is that defines our sport. For practical purposes, I have perhaps unwisely chosen to keep focused on *bouldering* movement, rather than speaking of the more general *climbing* movement, though without a doubt many of the ideas presented here apply to sport climbing, traditional and alpine climbing, etc. The reason for this is simple – sometimes, when you try to do too much, you don't do justice to anything.

David 'Buzz' Buzzelli deserves serious thanks for working through early drafts of this text, for enduring freezing winters on my home wall in my attic in Syracuse, and for being an incredible training partner. Buzz's knowledge of general athletics proved invaluable in numerous sections of this text. Thanks also to John Sherman for some helpful criticism, leads, photography, and overall structural issues. To various photographers, climbers, and artists, I owe a major thanks – their names appear in the credits. Ed Mooney of Syracuse University is responsible for planting the initial idea in my head, and so, Ed, thanks for that. A special thanks to my advisors for whom doing philosophy is a way of life – Jack Caputo, Gail Hamner, Carl Raschke and Patricia Cox Miller. A final thanks to Christy, Amelia, Francis IV, and my parents, Kate and Frank, for their support and love in all things.

Francis Sanzaro

⌘

NO STYLE NEEDED

The man who is really serious, with the urge to find out
what truth is, has no style at all.

Bruce Lee

To a boulderer, a problem is infinite in its own little way,
forever changing the way it greets us when we climb on it
or even look at it, never boring us with its fixed number
of holds but always opening toward us, always revealing a
new aspect of itself, and, conversely, of us. The slightest bit
of humidity (or frustration) can make a hard problem feel
impossible – whatever your limit is – just as a split tip can
set you back on attempts for days.

To boulder is to be put into a space that is, well . . . only
like bouldering, which is both obvious, and not. Once you
are hooked, a boulder is no longer a chunk of lifeless stone
but a giant apparatus to which we sacrifice our greatest
energies – something to which many, myself included,
devote years of prime physical strength. Contrived? Yep,
but what isn't?

In time, we are defined by the stone as much as it is
defined by us, by its speeds, textures, holds and behaviours;
our muscles and tendons adapt, bigger lats, bigger triceps
for mantels, or, equally, our bodies break, in which we are
defined by it much more. As sprinters of the climbing world,
no form of climber is as injury prone as the boulderer.

When we see boulders, we scrub, touch, inspect and
analyse every inch of their bodies, looking for a way up.
We search for a line to ascend, which will allow us to leave
our mark on the sport, something lasting, a first ascent. We
are looking for a creative act that will eventually produce a
performance that others can share and admire. Bouldering is

unique in that unlike a famous football goal or touchdown, the consequence of the first ascent of a boulder problem is a *publication* of its movement sequence, like putting down notes to a new song on paper so others can play it. This solution is postulated against the theses of other possible solutions; it is a brave thing, really.

Hopefully, we have found the unique sequence – since the success of our problem is often judged against other possible solutions (or lack thereof). A simple kneebar or a crimp a first ascensionist didn't see can significantly drop the grade – not an ideal scenario – bruising the ego, but, more importantly, indicating that they didn't look carefully enough. Fontainebleau bouldering sensei Charles Albert, who climbs barefoot, had his V17 downrated by two potential grades because Nicolas Pelorson found a better heel hook. Because we boulder with different bodies (morpho), bouldering will forever be a dance requiring reinterpretation. As it is with stone carving, so it is with bouldering – look five times, strike once.

We succeed to the point that others don't. That is, we succeed in cataloguing our brief performances into bouldering's archive when we are the first person to perform this movement. This act is both extremely solitary and public – a boulder problem's solution is ultimately found by an individual at a single point in time, yet its solution is often, but not always, a collaborative agreement born from a team mentality. Therefore, the boulder problem lives only insofar as it is remembered and memorialised by those for whom the act itself is of the utmost importance.

A problem is a short performance, lasting about a minute or two. Despite the prep and training and obsession, when you are bouldering at your limit, a hard send feels like a gift, often coming at the most improbable of times – at the end of a long session, for example, or on a 'rest day', or on your last try before you have to pack things up and drive home.

This was the case with Ben Moon's first ascent of *Black Lung* (V13, 8b) in Joe's Valley, which, in legendary fashion, he sent on his final go of the trip, after having packed up and gone for the car, only to turn around because the snow stopped and conditions got prime.

Bouldering will one day go extinct. Like the ancient and not-so-ancient sports of *Harpasta*, *Jeu de Paume*, *Equilibrium*, *Tug of Hoop* and *Trigon*, bouldering will no longer be part of the cultural imagination. Bouldering will no longer 'live', for sports have lifespans, like people. One day, the lights will be turned out inside the boulders themselves – the life they once had, which we boulderers gave to them so passionately, will die, and that vision and yearning we had for them will die as well, which isn't to say it was pointless, quite the opposite – all the more meaningful.

Before we 'found' them, boulders were anonymous faces of stone in varied landscapes – forests, mountains, valleys, neighbourhoods, Central Park – and we walked past them or simply marvelled at their shape and colour. Now they are apparatuses for the most brutal, pleasing, modern athleticism, a combination of art and instinct, max exertion, and softness. The combination of said skills is what it feels like to be in that bouldering space.

⌘

THE ART OF MOVEMENT

It takes an athlete to dance, but an artist to be a dancer.

Shanna LaFleur

Movement is not what we are doing, but movement is what happens in the event of bouldering. In bouldering, when the body is struggling, thinking and straining, movement is a third phenomenon, inhabiting a spectral presence between the body and the stone.

Movement is the expression of the meeting of these two bodies, just as speech is the result of air and the shape of the throat. In Chuck Fryberger's video portrait of Fred Nicole, a similar statement is offered about this third *happening* between two bodies. Speaking of his initial forays into bouldering, Nicole states: 'so it was nice to discover a type of climbing where I could just think about the climbing, the rock, myself, and movement.' As a medium, *it contains us* rather than us containing it.

In many ways, the myth of 'naturalness' or 'purity' in the sport of bouldering (that it requires such little equipment) has crippled the ability to think about our sport. Is not our movement just as contrived as any technology? Absolutely. Let's make no mistake about the contrivance of bouldering – the seemingly comical nature of its performance; the Herculean effort we exert on a small section of stone in the middle of a forgotten forest or valley or hill. The world couldn't care less for what we are doing, and its impracticality is to its benefit. But it is no more contrived than the 100m distance for sprinters, which is one of the most highly anticipated races in the world. They too (*they* being an amalgam of culture, spectators, history, etc.) quarantine the performative space, setting rigid boundaries within which an athletic pursuit can occur. In the sport of modern bouldering, we have been experiencing these definitional problems in numerous distinctions – highballing, traversing, the dyno, dab, the slab, standing start or sitting start, feet-on-for-full-points, etc. Each game has its rules.

Bouldering is *the* art of movement, so the story goes. It is climbing boiled down to its essentials: bare skin, chalk, rock shoes (or not), and if you remembered it, a brush. No clipping, no cumbersome rope, no yelling, no haul bag, no rack of draws. In bouldering, one is constrained by nothing but difficulty, nothing but moving on rock. The body must navigate nothing and consider nothing else but the labyrinth of movement itself. This, at least, is how bouldering has understood itself up until today. But it cannot claim the art of movement to itself – it is one of the many movement arts, and to *think* responsibly about bouldering is to think about it in combination with other movement arts.

One could say the same thing, for example, about dance – that it is the 'true' art of movement – and many have, rightly so. Journals, books, reviews and other narrative forms have given themselves to dance: dance theory, training, aesthetics, semiotics (theories of how dance creates meaning). Skim the shelves of any college library, and you'll find volumes dedicated to dance, the only *other* art of movement. Theorists at the top universities and the most brilliant choreographers in the world are at the cutting edge of pushing the body's limit in terms of dance and getting paid well to do so in the most expensive cities in the world and to audiences of thousands. Beneath marbled hallways and Baroque ceilings sporting gold-encrusted naves, newspaper and magazine critics line up to plum the hidden energies of what it is they just saw those dancing bodies do. Will bouldering ever be understood in this fashion? While the Tokyo Olympics will help, much depends on what is meant by 'art'.

Bouldering is indeed an art, but what constitutes the 'art-ness' in such a statement is not altogether obvious, aside from the oft-cited maxim that it takes creativity to figure out a boulder problem. It does, but that sells bouldering short. What exactly is our creativity? What is our modernity? These are the first questions we need to answer. The second thing we need to do is overcome the misconception that bouldering is about difficulty, which it isn't.

The two problems cannot be isolated from each other, for when we think bouldering is about difficulty, it loses, in direct proportion, its status as art. This problem is not unique to bouldering.

Like bouldering, during the past few decades, gymnastics has itself engendered a cult of difficulty, thanks to the appearance of the Russians in the 60s and 70s and, of course, the Cold War proxy rivalry. Transforming a once-fluid sport and replacing grace and charm with bone-breaking and tendon-stretching routines rewarded less the art of movement than the demonstration of its sheer impossibility. For example, watch a modern men's floor routine, and the sense of it isn't so much a unified whole, but rather a series of really hard tricks and skills with mediocre transitions. As a former gymnast, I'd know.

In terms of difficulty, the analogy in dance will see a performance where the performers try the most difficult moves without a pulse for agility or smoothness, two things we always expect from dance. We could never imagine a dancer simply jumping as high as he or she could or rotating as much as possible. That would feel brutish, and we, in our sports jacket and leather shoes, expect more from our dancers. We want to see beauty *and* brawn. We want our feats of strength packaged, hidden, as it were, under the mask of art; moreover, we want difficulty to be so flawless that it turns itself into something else – *grace*. And this is where the art of the body comes in.

Beauty is essential to the avant-garde quality of most performing arts, and it is crucial to bouldering, though we don't know exactly why. When one hears the word 'avant-garde', the original French for 'vanguard', attached to art or music, one should hear whispers of *the prophetic*. The dancer's body, like the athlete's, is an avant-garde body because it inspires in all its essential vagueness; it loves, leaps, twirls, and in turn makes us hope, inspires us, forces us to look at ourselves and aspire with it. The avant-garde prophesies a future state (cultural, political, religious, etc.) not yet achieved. It is embodied hope, realised impossibility and a present crystallisation of what we allow our public bodies to do. What we like our bodies to do today will certainly not be the case tomorrow – the extinction of many sports in history testifies to this.

We get dressed up and pay lots of money to witness fit bodies flop around the stage for hours because we believe that somewhere during the night we will see something special – something that required dedication, skill, energy, talent and love. This is why dance has an *industry*, an audience. Without viewers looking for these things, dance would cease to exist in public; it would be relegated to a dark basement – much like climbers in the 1990s, before gyms, when practitioners slaved away at perfection alone, or in the company of a few disciples. A place where, I might add, some would argue 'real' dance belongs.

But the lesson is this: something about the modern human body carries immanent to it all the hopes, fears, joys and accomplishments of modernity itself. Without a doubt, the structured positions, zoned territories and organised play of cricket, for example, captures the hierarchical aristocracy of English society, just as the curtsy has embedded within it gender roles no longer applicable to the 21st century, at least in Western liberalism. As movements of the body, sports are *gestures* like anything else, and they reflect broad cultural moods. For instance, Muhammad Ali's fluid bravado crystalised and asserted black political culture in America in the 1970s. They are like certain plants that can sprout, and thrive, only in particular habitats. Likewise, bouldering is an invention of our time, only of our time, and like other sports, it is in equal parts athletics, art and modernity.

THE ATHLETIC BODY

The athletic body has always been considered the ideal body. Encapsulated in the harmonious, fit and healthy body, we find the virtues of discipline, courage, fairness, hard work, dedication, passion and the strength to overcome adversity. The athletic body is much more than performance or entertainment – the athlete is a physical manifestation of moral and ethical values. What we value in our athletes is what we culturally value in general, or what we think we should value, regardless of whether we live up to the standards we expect of them. In fact, the less we can live up to the 'ideal' athlete, the more they are seen as superhuman, and therefore more worthy of adoration. This is, at least, the mythology of it all, earned or not.

Aside from today's athletes' celebrity status, which is troubling, athletes have since their Greek inception symbolised something more significant – an otherworldly being capable of superhuman feats, not to mention superhuman beauty. Athletes were god-like. Incredible athletes of the classical era were considered divine and worthy of royal tribute. Not much has changed. Athletes today remain repositories of social norms – modern-day 'icons' or 'examples to youth' – and when societies change, the athletes that once basked in public glory become buried as fossils which, once analysed, reveal a host of traits about a given culture.

An athlete, however, also acts. It is not just what the athlete *stands for*, but equally what it does, how it moves, how it performs. Even though the bulk of books and articles about athletics is social science and cultural anthropology, athletics is *about movement,* if it is about anything. It is about bodies in motion and what is happening inside those bodies. That is the essence of athletics since athletics consists of athletes, and athletes fail, succeed, get up, fall down, but, more importantly, they move.

On the other hand, athletics is informed by cultural trends. In America in the past few decades, we have witnessed the decline of boxing and the rise of MMA and UFC fighting. 'Fighting', as opposed to boxing, is understood to be much more creative, 'real' and violent, a sport that caters to the desensitisation of violence in America as well as the multicultural appetites for many martial arts styles, emblematic of our patchwork, multi-ethnic global culture. What goes for a fighter today is no longer the rounded, large-muscled body of an Ali, a Frazier or a Tyson, but the chiselled, leaner physique – quicker, more versatile, multi-dimensional and deadly.

Just as in boxing, where the ropes have been replaced by the 'cage', bouldering is a sport that has abandoned the stages and arenas of sport's history. The arena is replaced by the boulder 'field', 'cluster', or 'garden', to borrow a phrase from Gill. Skateboarding turns kerbs into athletic apparatuses, just as parkour does to the concrete landscape of urban life.

Boxing is changing into 'fighting' because it simply does not speak to, or for, its audience anymore. Yet athletes are not the only cultural figures that speak for generations. An analogy in music is the birth of the singer-songwriter in the late 1960s. Against a backdrop of big-band music and the decadence of the large stage came the lone musician carrying nothing but a guitar, three chords and a head full of poetry. This itinerant 'freedom-fighter', a concept so valued in the political climate of the 1960s, knew only the road and a confessional, intimate space of music. They had a story to tell, and people listened as if it were so. This is why people sat down in so many concerts while a musician was playing, which seems odd today. The practice spoke directly to an era valuing truth in both art and living, and it was the singer-songwriter that embodied the nexus between beatnik and counter-cultural activist.

This musical revolutionary could not have been 'born' ten years prior and could not be born today in the same manner. This 'musical body' was as much of its time as the bouldering body is of ours.

Timing, precision, balance and dynamism, such are the qualities bouldering shares with other sports, among others, but it has also broken new ground in the movement arts via a premium on compression, tension, contraction, momentum, etc.

Something unspeakable, something barely approachable, resides inside our sport, inside all athletics for that matter. It is the unaccommodating, uncompromising fact of movement itself – an entity not entirely of the rock, nor of our bodies, but a strange amalgam of the two. Bouldering movement is what happens when a body boulders. We cannot boulder without a rock, and the stone cannot boulder without us. Movement is defined by the alchemy of these two bodies – rock and flesh – and to understand it properly we must view it from various angles.

At its best, bouldering is that subtle skill that all athletics attempts to hone, in one way or another – the beauty of controlling the body during spectacular feats of strength, courage, impossibility and fear. It is an idealism we are chasing when we are bouldering at our finest. Bouldering is an act where our failures highlight the will/body split. That tiny gap – however minuscule and undetectable – reveals to us that, first, we are strangers to our own body and, second, the journey to remedy this alienation (athletics) is a profoundly joyous experience.

⌘

THE BOULDERING BODY

Learn the rules like a pro,
so you can break them like an artist.

Pablo Picasso

Insanity: doing the same thing over and over again and
expecting different results.

Albert Einstein

The bouldering body – gymnast, acrobat, stuntman – is always pushing the limits of the body's extremities. It is repeatedly asked to put him or herself in impossible scenarios. It is asked to read the situation immediately, travel, eat well, be disciplined, be self-motivated, train like an Olympian. Boulderers are strong yet lithe, like the martial artist, but don't muscle like the gymnast. Hard bouldering rarely rewards a gymnast's body, despite popular opinion, because we need to pull our weight up with our fingers, which might be unable to handle the bigger loads. Therefore, we focus on a type of strength imperceptible to a non-climber – finger strength.

Because bouldering is a game of finding limits, we are constantly expected to deal with failure, fall repeatedly, and learn from each failure. It is as if we believe in our collective unconsciousness that movement opens itself to the most dedicated, most disciplined, and of course, the most experimental. Which it does. For all its awkwardness, movement is a strange yet beautiful animal to inhabit.

We know never to get too attached to a sequence, that we must remain unfaithful to a single sequence until we are sure making the move a particular way will work when put in combination with other moves. In this manner, they are like mini routes since, after a few hangs, you might do the crux in an inefficient way. On a send go, totally pumped, that inefficiency will kill you every time; most of the time, bouldering is the same, just condensed. Like the creation of any multi-part composition, we must be aware of the entirety of the performance, and we need to manage our energies accordingly. A boulder problem doesn't just tell us how *it* wants to be climbed, it does to some extent, but we need to calibrate that sequence with our own fitness. In this way, it is more about common sense and confronting your own reality than anything. I've seen all too often climbers stubbornly refuse to change their beta because they are just too attached to it, for no particular reason, only to a month later send it first try with a new sequence. At its finest, bouldering teaches us about letting go, our false assumptions and what we are and aren't capable of doing – a cold bath in reality.

To boulder hard, you must exhibit absolute sobriety and cold-heartedness when it comes to not making foolish decisions. And yet, there comes the point in most boulder problems where one must detach oneself from all desires for control, self-mastery and self-preservation and let all the untapped resources of the body come forward in one instant, without conscious oversight or worry about injury. This is our creative moment.

Chuck Fryberger's sequence in *Core*, when introducing Nalle Hukkataival standing in the street with the world flashing neurotically around him, is very much an encapsulation of bouldering itself – silence amidst the noise of choice, too many options, too much *beta*. But this is what the boulderer must do – dissociate from the crew, the conversation, the debate over a sequence, and breathe, envision, and cultivate a new form of silence. The boulderer rarely screams – it is an art of silence – but when we do scream, it is the body's way of venting such that the other faculties of poise and patience can remain. It is akin to slowly unscrewing the top of a soda bottle, so the rest remains intact. Boulderers are expected to succeed repeatedly and never be satisfied, for our sport is organised so that it maintains provisional limits (such and such a problem), while its ultimate boundaries lie elsewhere. The nuances of failure seduce me every time, the reasons for failure never convincing enough to keep me from searching for the next problem, the next top out. Like an ever-receding horizon, no ultimate measuring stick can exist, and so, therefore, the boulderer is expected to move continuously towards the creation of new movements.

The bouldering body is an avant-garde body, communicating something new to us about our own cultural milieu. As a culture, we value athletic, emotional and physical attributes, all of which overlap: individuality, flexibility, adaptability, courage, counter-cultural idealism, self-determination, self-exploration, self-sufficiency.

Without knowing it, athletes are always at the forefront of a great, albeit unconscious, physical experiment. They are searching for the limits of human performance, the limits of the body, and what is amazing is that nothing motivates this tremendous cultural phenomenon other than the act itself. In fact, there wouldn't be athletics if there weren't *athletes*. The word *athlete*, Greek in origin, was reserved for those who 'contest for a 'prize'. It can be understood in many ways: a gold medal, accolades, fame and notoriety, but the real prize is the sensation of athletic mastery (the very thing we are chasing, whatever sport we are doing). This particular sensation, or affect, is the *raison d'être* of sport: jumping, climbing, running, *moving*. Competitions and prizes and medals are late to the evolutionary game.

Of course, there is money and sponsorship and commercials, but at the root of it all athletics is an automatic expression of being in a body, and it would cease entirely were it not the case. Regardless of its exposure, however arcane, each new athletic expression in culture is as valid as the most prized and popular. A contemporary sport, such as our own, says more about our current state of affairs than a sport played today but born two centuries ago.

It was no small feat for contemporary sports when in 2004 a few breakdancers made for their audience, Pope John Paul II. Something about how new, urban bodies danced on the pavement encapsulated something essential to modern life, something rebellious, creative, and expressive, or perhaps it was the plasticity of modernity itself. Yet it *was* a bit of modernity the Pope was keen to understand. Like bouldering, breakdancing had created a new, modern stage for its performance – not the field, not the arena, not the dome, but the floor.

So there it was, the Vatican with its gilded throne, coloured robes and conservative antiquity, contrasted with the whirling, fluid bodies of modern breakdancing, making the polished floors their ultimate space for art. It was about as political as athletic bodies get – a testament, perhaps, to the fact that bodily creativity will find a way to express itself when current means of expression are lacking or no longer available.

The avant-garde body pushes the limit of what a body can do, but, and this is a big but, it must do it with some element of beauty. Art interprets the past with an eye toward the future, and beauty (and ugliness) is the vehicle for delivery. While justified on many fronts, brute strength, whilst beautiful to many, removes the concept of performance from its act – strength is about strength, not about the display. A powerlifter should not be bothered by aesthetics. Brute force and pure exertion have an immediacy to them – a penchant for the non-reflective that performance cannot ignore. Bouldering may exist for a few as pure difficulty, all the grade chasers and whatnot, but it would not live as a sport if that were all it was, for sports are rarely about difficulty alone. Of course, to climb a hard boulder, you can't sacrifice efficiency for aesthetics either. To climb a hard boulder, your body is forced into an act that, by its very nature, requires the elements of beauty – flow, steadiness, poise, control, etc. – with the exception, of course, of that rare send where the climber is shaking and out of control.

In our films and videos, we boulderers demand and value a bit of art, a bit of grace and style, from our athletes. Smuggled especially into our sport, there is a core of art that we cannot escape. While beauty in rugby would be welcome, it is not a prerequisite, but it seems essential in bouldering. We don't want to see someone knee-scraping their way up a boulder – it does happen all the time, but it will rarely make it into a video. We want grace, and we want art; we want a polished send. Though art is not required of all sports, all sports benefit from a healthy dose of art. Bouldering straddles this boundary.

Another aspect separating a sport from art is competition. It needs to be said that it would be reckless for professional boulderers to consider beauty when climbing – they simply need to do the hardest problems, get the repeat, or the first ascent, or win the competition. Careers are on the line. Advertisers are lining up. Someone needs to get paid. But to focus solely on the sport's professionals is to miss what we value as *bouldering*. When we equate a sport with those who do it 'best', we have fallen victim to the logic of difficulty in modern sport. Those who can do *x* (*x* equals a difficult act) are merely doing their sport more intensely than others. Or, to put it another way, they are the best representatives. And sports are more than just catalogues of superhuman feats. Muhammad Ali may or may not have been the best boxer, but he sure came to represent the sport, as he should have; people loved him not just for his personality but also for the way he bounced, flowed, defended, and created opportunity inside the ring.

As in the Japanese tea ceremony, it is not about difficulty but about using that ceremony (or performance) to get you somewhere. Those who climb V15 (Font 8c) are no more privileged to this performative space than those who climb V8 (7b+). We think bouldering is about difficulty because we are focusing on those doing the most difficult things. This may be due to the effect of the media, no doubt, as well as a fascination with what a body can ultimately do. Of course, many of us don't believe this is the case. The vast majority climb for fun, choss around on low and mid grades, and don't worry about sending their project every time they chalk up.

⌘

THE STAGE

The boulder becomes a surreal gymnastic apparatus
. . . the focus is on specific movements and their difficulty,
and connecting these individual moves together.

Ivan Greene

Have we found a sophisticated way of speaking about our sport? Why has so much been written about dance and virtually nothing about bouldering? The most obvious answers are as follows: dance has a stage; dance has an audience; dance has professors; dance is in bed with universities; people pay a lot of money to watch it; dance has history and culture, and empires have supported it as a flag of their achievement, such as the Russians. The body and ethereal movements of Anna Pavlova, perhaps the most celebrated of all Russian ballet dancers, was said to be the flowering of the charm, sophistication, and achievement of the 'Silver Age' of Russian culture. Working for the Russian Imperial Ballet at the beginning of the 20th century, it was said that her overarched feet symbolised the highest aspirations of the Russian people.

Dance usually takes place on a flat floor that gives itself to the production of abstract principles and concepts. This *tabula rasa* allows an absolute starkness to the dancing body that gives itself to theory and philosophy. This clean slate presents a (false) conception that it is an activity without limitation, that is, radical, bodily freedom. As the idea would go, dance creates *something from nothing* – an original act of creation ex nihilo, in the biblical sense of Genesis. Therefore, these pure bodies can generate higher artistic content – ideals to be exact – while the *other* athletes supposedly produce no such ideals but only acts. Artists produce meaning from nothing; athletes struggle with pre-existing material.

The 'purity' of the dance stage – its 'lack' of an apparatus or bulky equipment – entices critical reflection because thought is tricked into believing that the dancer's body is unconstrained, and therefore this freedom is opposed to the labour of sport. Athletes grunt. Dancers fly. Athletes sweat. Dancers glide. A labourless activity no doubt has class and economic implications and truly highlights that 'cultural sports' are those for upper-class consumption. In any case, dance movements are interpreted as self-imposed and self-willed, and so therefore artistic. They overcome nothing but self-limitation, and, in this manner, the notion of ultimate creation is retained to keep the mythos of the genius-artist alive. This is why athletics is not considered high art. But this theory is flawed.

John Gill did not invent bouldering, but he has, more than any other, detailed the sport's long and storied history. According to Gill, bouldering – understood as a practice of ascending hard lines on boulders or cliff lines – had begun around the mid-to-late 1800s. For the most part relegated to training mountaineers and alpinists, it would remain a subterranean sport until the decades following Gill's early years, around the 1950s, through to the 1970s, when we can begin to recognise the first manifestations of the sport we now know today. It was only once it became detached from alpine-climbing culture that it could open itself to the larger trends of modernity. It was only then that larger cultural trends invaded the practice of ascending boulders.

One could never imagine a professor being trained in 'bouldering theory', though the thought experiment is interesting. For all these reasons stated above, and many more, bouldering will most likely never have a culture or literature. More importantly, its practitioners will never be seen to represent the highest art of any given culture. Chris Sharma will never be to America what Vaslav Nijinsky was to Russia, and yet, figures like Tony Hawk broadcast a specific brand of Americanism across the globe even while more prominent images, such as that of Michael Jordan dunking a basketball, encapsulate the supposed freedom, athletic and racial, of American society.

In China, the famous image of Michael Jordan dunking the ball from the foul line, with his tongue out on full display, was said to represent the power and freedom granted to Westerners (and minorities) in liberal democracies, something that many Chinese still desire. Bodies are always political, even national, highlighted again by the body of Stallone in *Rocky*, whose muscle is earned the 'natural way' – lifting rocks, chopping wood, running in the snow, sweat, dirt, potatoes. Good ol' fashion, hard-earned muscle. Rocky is pitted against Drago's body – the machinic body of Russia, whose penetrating technologies will stop at nothing to increase the calibre of their athletes. But there it was, the Cold War proxy fight symbolised in bodies: wholesome America, whose strength came from nowhere but a rugged moral imperative, versus the body of Russia, whose blank and emotionless stare lacked a soul, and whose power came not from an inner will but through the scientific-technological apparatus. Not that any of these depictions are accurate, since American athletes are some of the most plugged-in of any in the world. It's just that the bodies 'promoted' are heavily marked by virtues either present in or desired by the same culture.

While bouldering might never become a fine art, it *can* have a language, and it *can* have concepts that are unique to its movement and style. It is about time. Admittedly, most sports, such as football and basketball, lack a critical and philosophical architecture. This lack is more an attribute of how we choose to look at a given sport than the sport itself.

While figure skating has a rink, bouldering happens in patches of forests, mountains, and valleys by mostly unknown, counter-cultural gipsies, and, of course, yuppies and everyone in between. We shamelessly set up camp in nearby patches of land or on the parking lot. Bouldering requires little formal 'training' and is often never witnessed by the public. Moreover, it is antisocial, having embraced a 1970s road trip, Camp 4, 'dirtbag' culture. It borders on an anti-capitalist, anti-societal philosophy, promoting lifestyle over 'career'. Thanks to Kauk, Long and Bachar, and more recently, to Sherman.

From the 1970s, conservative-era perspective, such dirtbaggers represented everything that was 'wrong' with society – long hair, unemployment, loitering, homelessness – while today, 40 years later, *sans* the long hair, the itinerant lifestyle remains intact. However, #Vanlife has since complicated that integrity. While the growth of a cult of climbing grew in America to the beat of a vastly different political era, the subtext of the lifestyle continues. It continues despite the co-opting of our sport by extreme sports industries and alternative *Generation X* media.

Unlike the so-called 'lost', apathetic, and nihilistic younger generation of slackers popularly known as *Generation X* – a term coined in the 1950s by the photographer Robert Capa – which is said to have provided the cultural milieu behind the emergence of bouldering (among other contemporary sports like parkour, surfing and skateboarding), today's boulderers are defined in the positive/active – the professional boulderer is marked by ceaseless travel and constant production: sending, cleaning, first ascents (FAs), sending, travelling, sending again.

The bouldering-developer has assumed the mantel of the 20th-century capitalist. They scan the territory, pursuing the most efficient means towards production. They fly around the world, most of the time on their sponsor's dime, and produce media. They provide products (boulder problems) that are (sometimes) meant to be shared. They provide market access to their product through media, mostly social media, whose followings and likes earn them money, often through crude formulas. They earn street credibility, money, or whatever it is, in the process of online videos, guidebook production, etc. Early climbing videos, such as in the 1990s through to around 2010, tended to be regional and national, focusing on the athlete doing hard things, and occasionally the road trip. However, since climbing is now global and included in the Olympics, there is more often a social advocacy angle to many climbing videos.

Bouldering media works just like any other media production – it has cycles of focus (certain areas are 'in'). As new places are discovered, new media cycles begin, and the old sites fall out of the limelight. With an increasing reliance on a shared stock of hard problems – such as the hard classics in Rocky Mountain National Park (*Centaur, Jade, Nothin' But Sunshine*, etc.), or Ticino, or Stanage – assuring access to those areas ensures the reputation of strong climbers. Such sites are also the fields on which we play and the grounds on which climbers rise and fall in the pecking order. Ticking off problems is essential for the modern boulderer, and only a few strong climbers push the limit of what's possible without constant media exposure.

Boulder problems (and routes) are commodity-experiences we consume according to our desires. A climbing gym sells routes. These are their products, and on this route is an experience, which is why setters in the U.S. and Europe are well paid and highly respected. Bouldering is at the nexus of the post-modern condition of choice, identity, and limit, as there is always a problem that suits your style. Boulder problems present choices to the consumer-athlete. It is easy to 'fail' on a problem when it is not your style.

⌘

FIELDS, CLOCKS, COACHES

> For boxing really isn't a metaphor, it is the thing in itself.
> Joyce Carol Oates

Bouldering represents a large-scale dissatisfaction with our dads' games: sports contained by fields, clocks, coaches, rules, and balls. It is no coincidence that bouldering connects us with the outdoors when the environment is receding like an ageing hairline. However, we cannot deny that just as bouldering often takes us into wild places, the wildness of the place is frequently diminished the more a place gets developed – as more climbers go there, parking lots expand, and with that comes access problems. Human activity threatens wildlife; footfall is a problem, etc. This situation is not improved with a generation of boulderers growing up in the gym then going outside and treating it as such, which is not always the case.

Talk of climbing's spiritual side almost always drudges up the undercurrents of natural temporality – *being* in the mountains, *spending* time in nature, *observing* the wild. Surfers, mountaineers, and kayakers, among many others, talk in the same manner, but, lest we forget, there is nothing natural about any of these sports. Bouldering, like kayaking or fishing or surfing, is also made possible by advances in technology: material compounds and plastics design; sticky rubber, down jackets (for hard sending in cold temperatures; the same goes for Gore-Tex's revolutionary effect on alpinism), sweat-wicking chalk, Google Maps for finding long-hidden boulder fields; and advances in accessibility, population development (accessibility and trails); leisure and 'First World' wealth (how many internationals at the boulder fields come from 'Third World' countries?); cheap building materials (climbing gyms in glorified warehouses in suburbia). Sadly, we are too optimistic in thinking that the development of bouldering areas redeems them and that it is the boulder field's desire to be developed by us. They don't. The boulders don't need us, we need them, and we should never forget this. A patch of forest no more desires to be enveloped in concrete than a boulder wishes to be stripped of moss and covered with chalk.

While outdoor bouldering is generally done in solitude, the industry has created the *simulacrum* (or copy) of bouldering in the form of indoor gym competitions, though outdoor competitions exist as well. Bouldering has a split nature: it is internally divided between 'plastic' and 'outdoors', but this schizophrenia is only superficial – bouldering is about a specific type of movement and the affect it produces in a body, regardless of the delivery device. Few sports have such a divide: surfing is coastal, and there is no practical way to surf in simulation with any bit of seriousness. Artificial waves do exist, and they are getting more dialled by the day, but this does not mean most surfers have access to them or will anytime soon. Creating indoor gyms and competitions has allowed bouldering to become sustainable, which allows for increased marketing of 'the product'.

In his writings, when researcher and professor Kyle Kusz described the general tendencies of modern, extreme sports as individual, risk-taking, fostering innovation and creativity, he could just as easily be describing bouldering. Along with our modernity, an anti-capitalist sentiment still marks the sport today, and we would be the worse for it if we were not to retain its original spirit of rebellion and anarchy. Though he is speaking of sport climbing, the late Wolfgang Güllich specifically mentioned the contribution that Camp 4 added to climbing. Güllich wrote: 'Sport climbing is, in part, defined by the lifestyle it engenders.'

According to Güllich – something that any German intellectual would point out due to the prevalence of Marxist thought in the country – the type of movement this lifestyle promotes has class consequences. Of course, Güllich does not deny the importance of climbing performance, only that it differs from mainstream sports in the alternative, counter-cultural lifestyle it encourages. It is a means of self-determination, self-realisation, and expression in contrast to careerism and corporatism – two elements that define the West in the 21st century. Bouldering is a middle- to lower-class phenomenon in which one can find as strong an identity as football or insurance sales. It is a means of escape, a remedy. And it would seem ludicrous for a young professional to quit their job to travel abroad to play soccer in foreign fields without the hope of becoming a professional, just to 'kick around' the ball, yet this is precisely what climbers do (and skiers, paddlers, surfers, and a few others for that matter). They are often called 'lifestyle sports', which is partly true except when the phrase is used to connote that it is an accessory, just some type of athletic-capitalist, image-based 'purchase'.

Sport and life are hard to separate in these disciplines. Some sociologists attribute the growth of contemporary lifestyle sports to the loss of traditional anchors of identity – job, family, marriage – with some going as far as to claim that they grew in the wake of insecure masculinity in the 70s: children of Baby Boomers rejecting the comfort-seeking behaviour of their parents; failures in warfare resolution (Vietnam); racial equality and gender equality; and inequality in income levels.

As climbing goes to the global 'market' via the Olympics, there are no doubt schizophrenic tendencies it will need to work through, hence all the talk of climbing 'losing its soul'. Even in his own time, in the 80s and 90s, Güllich admitted that 'careers, money and social prestige are becoming the centre of interest'. Though taking part in some of the earliest competition, Güllich quickly pulled away from competitions, in part citing what they were, and would, do to climbing. As he foresaw, 'professionalism' and standardisation create new, often unwelcome, dynamics in our sport, and the trend continues. The influx of money and professionalism into bouldering will change it, and these growing pains can be seen in the 'uncut footage' debate so that a climber can prove an ascent (such as in the case of Said Belhaj or Rich Simpson). The same can be found in the use of GPS coordinates for alpinists (Ueli Steck and others). The argument for proof is that top-end climbers now agree that to claim a hard ascent or hard boulder, you need uncut footage or reliable witnesses. As it should be.

⌘

GILL

There are no secrets to becoming strong. It's all about hard work. Beer and women will be the ruin of you.

Ben Moon

While many people think that modern bouldering is concerned with difficulty and credit John Gill with its inception – he introduced chalk to our sport and sent V9 in the 1950s, for instance – it's forgotten that Gill was never after difficulty for its own sake. Rather, he pursued a *bodily state of affairs*, a particular affect. He was after a mood. Bouldering achieved that.

In an interview, Gill writes: 'Remember, I had a peculiar agenda that did not focus entirely on getting up problems that others could not. What felt kinaesthetic was what I liked to do. Contorting into a yoga position on the rock just to get up didn't appeal to me.' Which is also to say, while anything could have sufficed, such as running, dance, track or gymnastics, nothing else did. Bouldering provides a very specific emotion – nothing philosophical here: it is simply the way the bouldering body moves that induces certain states in the body. Tennis has its own 'branding' on the body in terms of affect, which cannot be replicated by throwing the javelin. The same goes for bouldering.

In the 1950s and 1960s, Gill travelled with a few friends, more often alone, and sent hard boulder problems before they could be called *problems*. Like California-native Jeff Clark surfing the monster waves of Mavericks alone, for a decade, before the break got notoriety, Gill pioneered, and thrived, in relative obscurity – for the simple love of it. Difficulty surfaced by default, first because of history and second because bouldering transitioned from arcane practice to public sport, the latter seen already in Gill's lifetime.

Gill did have a grading system like ours today (the V-scale, for example, or the European Font-scale), but the difference between them cannot be overestimated. Gill's B1-B3 system was fundamentally based on ascents, not necessarily difficulty, though he did intend for it to be objective, and, of course, he was trying to climb hard. For Gill, a B1 contained a move that was the hardest move on a rope done at the time, such that many people could do it. B2 was harder than that. B3 was really hard, repeated only once or twice, or, if more than that, it would become B2.

True, ascents have much to do with difficulty. The fewer the repeats, the more difficult they are, yet a scale of difficulty attempts to be objective about the body's capacity, or incapacity, to pull off sequences of moves. The burden of proof for a scale of difficulty is the stone itself and what it provides – analogous to the measuring stick in the high jump – as opposed to Gill's system that merely registered the difficulty based on repetition. Gill's system naturally slides as bodies and training become more efficient (his system was very broad except for the grades at the higher end of the scale). Modern systems attempt to catalogue what the rock provides – we know what the rock provides judged on how our bodies react to it.

The reclusive boulderer-prodigy myth has its origins on the Front Range of Colorado. With names like Gill, Jim Holloway and a few others, the stage was set for stories of incredible feats of strength with equally incredible amounts of solitude. So it's no wonder that Holloway is still something of an urban legend: exactly how strong he was, what he could do today, and so on. *Did he really climb V13 (8b) in the 1970s?* Gill himself was an avant-garde figure, a man of prophetic movement, a figure in the fiction of bouldering that caused countless others to keep pushing their bodies towards the edge of what is possible. Holloway stands next to Gill in terms of mythical status, and James

Litz is a modern example of the myth of the strongman cultivating his strength on a secluded chunk of rock, with no idea of how his problems compared to others.

For my generation of *Rocky* viewers, myself included – equal part Cold War mentality coupled with an American penchant for the lonely Cowboy – these heroes fed the myth of the solitary bouldering genius whose strength, like their problems, may perhaps forever remain unknown. But the sport is so public today that such private feats, even if kept as secretive as possible, rarely go unpublished; these climbers are caught too early to be so naive as to climb V15 (8c) without a press-kit. Like all sports that go corporate, the logic of capitalism necessarily follows – speed of execution becomes more valued than depth of experience. Difficulty replaces the joy of movement.

Perhaps this is what we are doing when we 'tick' an area and move on – appreciation is lost, for what value is there really (irony here) in returning to a site to repeat the problems we have already done when we could go and tick new ones? We have been turned into hyper-consumers.

⌘

FLASH, RAMPAGE, FUTURE

A great phenomenon of bouldering is the *rampage* – referring to the rare and decisive success that a boulderer has when visiting a new area. Aptly the title of a video by Josh Lowell in 1999, the term speaks volumes about the nature of our sport: how specific achievements are met and by what standards professional boulderers are set apart from the rest. No doubt a consequence of postmodern globe-trotting, increasing levels of sponsorship money, ease of travel and accessibility of boulders, the rampage marks a climber's ability to dispatch a large number of hard boulder problems in a relatively short time in a new area. Moreover, it also indicates a certain plateau of difficulty and how we have come to value climbers' achievements.

In 1900 the best-recorded jump was just under 25ft (7.61m), by Peter O'Connor of Dublin. Today, it is around 29ft (8.95m). A hundred years for 4ft! Impressive, no doubt, but in the age of steroids, larger gene pools and better training regimes, we expect more, right? I'd bet we'll never jump another 4ft past our current record. Without question, climbing will not see the same exponential growth, and we will see long lulls in the sport where the record is not broken. Perhaps we will see the occasional micro-improvement, akin to Usain Bolt's 2009 100m sprint world record, in which he shaved off 16-100ths of a second to put the current record at 9.58s. Remarkably, the time between Usain Bolt and the person who has run the 1,000th fastest time is around half a second. And in 1912, almost exactly a hundred years ago, Usain Bolt would have beaten American sprinter Donald Lippincott by a mere second. Lippincott ran the 100m in 1912 in 10.6 seconds. One hundred years for one second over the space of a hundred yards. When things begin to even out, much in the way the record in javelin or discus or pole vault is only occasionally beaten, and if it is only by inches, we will put much more emphasis on flashing a problem. Like the rampage, flashing a problem will determine a climber's immediate level, as opposed to their ability after working a problem for a long time. The flash will determine how well a boulderer knows the nature of stone.

The rampage is typically confined to one area. Its remarkable achievement attests to the difficulty of internalising new forms of stone, i.e. adapting to the idiosyncratic qualities that each venue provides. In *Pure*, Nalle Hukkataival speaks of the technical attributes of Fontainebleau's problems, remarking that it takes a longer time to solve them. A case in point is that Ondra, who has flashed V15 (8c), sent 5.15d and sent a handful of V16s (8c+), fell on a V2 (6a) in Font. Jerry Moffatt in *The Real Thing* comments on how the holds in Fontainebleau ('Font') require that technique be defined not in terms of how you grip the hold but how you position your body on the hold. Ondra can discourse for hours about the idiosyncrasies of the friction and technique required in some areas as opposed to others. This is also why some climbers can tick V15 (8c) in their home area but go abroad and get shut down – they just cannot translate their strength and technique to new rock.

For example, boulderers at Hueco require agility in the fingers to position themselves perfectly on the incuts. And without the ability to stand on polished nubs for feet, a hard boulderer from Yosemite will have to settle for moderates. Quickly able to dig deep into the repertoire of movement at their disposal, the skilled boulderer shortens the usual time it takes to adjust to new boulders; this should be the goal of all of us. While a gymnast has to push difficulty on an unchanging apparatus, and a football player navigates an unchanging apparatus with the added variables of changing bodies, the boulderer has to encounter new movement on a changing apparatus.

Whereas for most boulderers the breaking-in phase can take months or weeks, to enter an area and dispatch its hardest lines is perhaps the most challenging feat in bouldering that we have. Even harder than the random, hard flash or ticking something at your limit in your home area. Today's World Cups test this very same adaptability with its variety of problems. A typical comp with four problems will have some slabs, for instance, and in the Meiringen 2019 World Cup the setters added a hand-jam, which, for obvious reasons, shut down the vast majority of climbers, all of whom never learned the technique. Naturally, Ondra cruised it, an all-rounder.

A single objective guideline for measuring climbers against each other is not available to us. Leading American route-setter Chris Danielson says that variety is the only way to separate climbers: 'We want first and foremost to split the field of competitors fairly. We hope that their performance on a variety of climbs will show, through a balance of power and fitness, mental tenacity, route-reading and on-sight ability, which among them is the best.' Adaptability, quick mastery and instinct are valued over memorising a routine, brute strength, or the deployment of a set of skills that carry a preordained difficulty value. Coordination, timing jumps, full-body harmony – the top competitors today have mastered these arts.

Gill was known early for his rampages in the boulder 'gardens' beneath popular climbing areas, and it was here that Pat Ament notes that 'Gill left a mysterious presence that climbers local to each area respected.' A quote that begs the question: what exactly is being left behind?

Bouldering is social, but in essence, a boulder problem is an intimate affair, and every boulderer should have at least one problem that is a secret, one you get on alone, at night. For me, it exists in a deep wash in the foothills of

Fort Collins, surrounded by purple and orange and crusted yellow granite. A small stream meanders its way among the boulders, and tall grasses keep you hiking in the streambed for fear of snakes; stubborn green shrubs and sage line the brown, dusty earth and hawks constantly patrol the ridges and valleys.

It's not that I want to keep a secret, but the inviolable revelation reveals, more cryptically, the nagging sense that not all moves need to be made public. More specifically, it brings up the idea that movement itself can be very personal, almost secretive. Often, when we succeed on a move, to try to say what exactly it is we are doing is extremely difficult. We climb in public, among hikers, gawkers, other boulderers, friends, strangers, and animals, and yet sometimes when I move, I do not want an audience. I need no witness, no publication of my ascent; it is as if the presence of other eyes cataloguing the beta robs me of its privacy, memorialises it out of its fleeting nature. In other words, the movement gets published, and I didn't want to write anything.

When working problems, we memorise and analyse each detail, foothold, and chip. We need to. Bouldering brings the body to a unique paradox – that of memory and the memorial. A strict and disciplined process binds us to the properties of a boulder problem – we must inhabit it so profoundly that it mentally and physically scars us, leaves its mark. Of course, many would count one's wounds as trophies, but I've known countless climbers for whom sending their project leaves them with postpartum depression. For mountaineers, sport climbers, it's all the same – when you've put so much time and energy into something, and then it's over, you experience a sense of loss. For some, the moment they get close to sending something is when things get serious and, unable to take the sport 'seriously'. They shut down, move to another problem, or concoct a vast story of doubt, trying to convince you and others that the very nearness of success testifies to their inevitable failure. All the shades of psychology insert themselves there. Perhaps they are intelligently avoiding the trappings of bouldering success. To be working something is easy. To be close to sending something and then send it is astonishingly hard.

⌘

VISIONS OF EXCESS

To dance is to challenge the body which is also the self. To generate an action which has a force of its own and allow the movement to penetrate the inner sensibilities, or to calculate the action and try to tune out – this is difficult, perhaps possible.

Katherine Litz

For me, the photo of John Gill's one-arm lever – a move I've been attempting unsuccessfully for years – encapsulates the essence of modern bouldering, and by default, contemporary athletics in general. Why? Because it is in excess of all necessity to bouldering. I'd be willing to bet that the strongest climbers in the world cannot do this, and I have yet to see a climber pull it off, though there are plenty of YouTube vids of the feat. Why then did Gill do it? In an article titled, 'The Art of Bouldering', Gill provides some clues as to the role of this strength: it adds a bit of grace. All that for grace?

This image is also the image of training. *Excess* is the name I will give to this image, though many others are apt. Why excess? It so far exceeds what an ordinary body is capable of – or what a climber needs – that it puts normal bodies in stark relief, not to mention inferiority. Excess has much to do with expectation –expecting an act in any athletic performance when all variables cannot be foreseen. Excess allows one to smooth over the unforeseen trials of expectation.

We train to latch onto certain holds. Gill's feat on *The Thimble*, which for years went unrepeated, is in part due to specific training – doing pull-ups on half-inch bolts, which are damn hard. This adaptive training of Gill's allowed us to increase the calibre of the athlete that our sport attracts and the type of power that those athletes must possess.

In his now-classic article, Gill recommends fingertip pull-ups, slow muscle-ups and one-arm levers: 'The ability to perform all these exercises is not absolutely essential to bouldering. However, the display of these skills often adds a certain polish or finesse to one's climbing and most really excruciating boulder problems generally demand certain special strengths of this nature.'

Quite the opposite of the rampage, in which a boulderer quickly adapts to a new area, the hardest boulder to date is Nalle's *Burden of Dreams* (V17/9a), which resides in his home country and took him years and dozens upon dozens of days of projecting. When Nalle wasn't on the boulder, he was working the moves via an indoor replica. Ondra did the same thing for the kneebar and V15 (8c) 'crack' crux of *Silence* – he replicated them at a home wall so that when he did go back, the move was catalogued into his muscular nervous system, and it would be that much easier. Eager to get the second ascent of the world's hardest problem, still unrepeated as of early 2021, Japanese climber Ryohei Kameyama poured a compound over the holds of *Burden of Dreams* and went home and had those exact holds made and reconstructed the problem. This technology of replication is, in many ways, doing for outside problems with the MoonBoard did for indoor climbing, which is make it such that climbers around the world can bring a problem home.

Later in his article Gill notes that perhaps a boulderer's most efficient deployment is in the success of completing dynamic movements – the *toss, lunge, dyno, deadpoint, huck,* or *triple,* the latter a series of three interconnected coordination moves commonly seen in World Cup problems. Bouldering requires dynamic moves – they signal that the body wants to overcome itself. Dynamism signals that the body wants to break the shell that points-on movement has constructed (where excess strength allows one to perform these moves). Gill is right to locate this excess of strength in moments of controlled grace. Here the discussion revolves around stabilisation and management of violent exertion, an observation that locates such displays of strength exactly at the point when the brute-ness (the obviousness) of one's strength is concealed – concealed, that is, by the spectacle of the dyno. In moments of violent exertion, control and poise are attributes of performance that the Greeks thought made the perfect athlete. Paradoxically, the spectacle of the move hides the strength of the body. Yet, the move is made possible only by excess strength, precisely how climbing is often perceived in popular competitions: equal parts circus act and technical precision, both acrobat and stuntman. Daniel Woods is phenomenal in this regard, his precision and control hiding what is just below the surface: max effort.

Are not competition problems distillations of the fantasy of bouldering, just as football movies fantasise ideals of football? Do our indoor competitions reveal what we think is *really* going on inside the core of bouldering – dynamic, dramatic flourishes of bodily extension caught between moments of mind-numbing interpretation? Crowd-pleasing, jaw-dropping, anti-intuitive, panic-inducing, showboating, beautiful, silent, opaque. It is as if the moves come out to the light, as if someone had put a flashlight into the bouldering body and turned the dial, taken what was implicit and made it explicit. The germ of movement is expressed in these dramatic stagings, and bouldering expresses its postmodernity in the bodily flamboyance of competitions. It is no coincidence then that Josh Lowell, in *Progression,* dramatically pans his camera onto the giant stage for a sport-climbing competition as if to hint at something essential, something hidden in climbing that the stage, there, under the lights, is going to reveal.

Gill likens the connection to a gymnastic performance, and it is no doubt gymnastics that Gill finds most akin to the 'summitless' scrambling that he was doing, which was later called bouldering. Gymnastics caught Gill's imagination regarding grace under pressure, what gymnasts call 'form'. The form of a gymnast's body, I know, having been one myself, is not a noun but an index of his power. Power is measured by the ability to sustain muscular exertion and balance under intense conditions. Form is a pointed toe and a smile during a Maltese or Victorian Cross, and power allows him to do so. Form (and difficulty) is that *through which* a gymnast is primarily scored, yet it is more precise to say that form is how difficulty is managed. Form is yogic in that correct form is success; grace is an attribute of form.

Is a man bench-pressing a thousand pounds graceful when his arms shake and his face turns red? Most would say no – his movement is utilitarian. Basketball is not a sport of grace, yet there are graceful players. Show jumping is graceful but is trick-orientated. Is bouldering a sport of grace? As of the modern era, yes and no. Much depends on how we define success. Gill may have been on the mark when he wrote the following: 'In bouldering, you're concerned as much – if not more – with form, style, elegance and route difficulty as you are with getting to the top.' Is he right?

If a gymnast attempts to inhabit a type of form created before them via gymnastic tradition, such as the prerequisite that a Maltese Cross must be done with pointed toes, the boulderer attempts to inhabit a type of form dictated by the rock. Our 'tradition' isn't informed by culture, as gymnastics is, but rather geology. Posture, body position, getting just the right smear for a heel hook – these are all types of forms over which the boulderer should obsess, and he or she should drop all moves that don't work, despite how beautiful they might be.

Getting into (and out of) 'form' is how we succeed. Shifting in and out of multiple forms is the boulderer's art, but unlike gymnastics, we use form as a means to an end, not the end itself. Trying to make a case for bouldering as a sport in-itself, Gill writes:

One might be led, from these comments, to the conclusion that bouldering is simply practice climbing for the expert, but there is more substance to the sport than that. Bouldering provides informal competition similar to the more formal variety found in artistic or competitive gymnastics. The comparison is quite appropriate moreover, since both activities require that extremely difficult body manoeuvres be performed in a graceful manner. This analogy illuminates a novel aspect of bouldering: the boulderer is concerned with form almost as much as with success and will not feel that he has truly mastered a problem until he can do it gracefully.

Things have changed. Sure, we repeat problems, and we master them, but do any of us work on grace? Who would really in their right mind try to suss a graceful sequence for a V9 (7c) rather than send their V12 (8a+) project? Perhaps Gill was both ahead of his time and out of his time – 'out' of his time because already 'ahead'. But it can't be denied that all climbers have a circuit of warm-ups at their local area, and, at least speaking for myself, I always try to improve on those circuit boulders each time I get on them. Why? Because the feeling of mastery, of grace, is a sensation unlike no other. Gill is right that we can't master a problem until we do it gracefully.

In gymnastics, the apparatus is more stable, less finicky. Though rock is solid, the point is not to fall off. Hanging on is not the goal in gymnastics; one does tricks through, around and on the apparatus. By tradition and culture, the apparatus is pre-chosen to be an appropriate tool for exercising certain skills. Change the diameter of the men's high-bar, and you will eventually see different tricks being executed and others go extinct. With a thicker high-bar, certain release moves would become nearly impossible due to the inability to catch a wider bar, given that the gymnast must wrap his fingers around the bar and get a good grip to prevent him from hitting the mat after a huge release move.

Apparatus dictates movement. The outdoor boulder can never be designed in this manner, though the indoor problem follows the same logic as a gymnastics apparatus. As any setter knows, the difference between a hard problem and an impossible problem comes down to these minor variations, such as the degree of a sloper, the lack of a thumb, the width of a pinch, etc.

What separates bouldering from gymnastics is that 'success' is clearly demarcated. As an ex-gymnast, a gymnastic routine is never perfect, regardless of what the score might say. You always feel you could have done better. A routine needs to be executed on a pre-set model to which the gymnast conforms – success is measured in terms of execution. Any deviation from this model means a deduction in points. A boulderer may make as many mistakes as they like, as long as they get to the top. For most of us, success is the top. The issue reminds me of surfing. They have 'V10' waves, waves where the take-off is steep and fast and requires more skill than a crumbly roller, but surfing is more of an affective sport, one of internal kinesiology rather than difficulty. With the exception of the beginner, just *finishing* the wave is not enough. Often, success for surfing is an index of style – style rules all and the best surfer has the most of it. Good style feels better through the affective experience (stoke, flow, etc.) given to the body. The *product is the process*, one might say. Dancers no doubt agree. Crucially, style is now understood as an achievement in its own right rather than as an appendix to the body. Babe Ruth had style, but it didn't make him famous. The same can't be said for snowboarders, skateboarders, or surfers.

⌘

GRACE AND TRUTH

It is not altogether obvious why bouldering has ended up the way it has, but one thing is sure – the brand of movement that we have collectively selected as difficult can mostly be achieved only through grace. Which is not to say that grace is always required – *just most of the time.*

Why is that? We have created an activity that is, at its most fundamental layer, joyful. Joy must be the *a priori* condition of possibility in bouldering – joy that is produced by the body but one which the body captures from its own movement. Two theses: joy comes before the desire for difficulty, and athletics are cultural expressions of bodily joy. We begin climbing out of joy and progress through it. It accompanies us the entire way. And bouldering is subservient to joy, not difficulty.

That mysterious item, then, found on the bodies of our best boulderers, attached to their movements like wet to water, well, it is a peculiar trait called 'grace'. An old term bequeathed to us and about as ambiguous as 'truth', or 'substance' or 'essence' – terms that philosophers to this day still struggle to define. To be graceful is not to master the odds of defeat; it is to *excel in them.* Grace is like beauty – you know when you are in the presence of it but wouldn't dare say you've found it once and for all. Ben Moon's grace is much different from Paul Robinson's, or J.B Tribout's or Alex Megos'. Each one embodies it for only a fleeting moment – on the pinch move on Bishop's *Lucid Dreaming* or the crux move on the Frankenjura's *Action Directe* – just enough for it to be lost before we think we have found it. Another boulderer picks it up for a bit, displays it, and drops it off again into the pit. We take part in it; we embody it, channel it, allow it to flow into us, but it is not easy. Grace is one of the hardest things to embody. Just as we cannot go out and perform one of Martha Graham's dance pieces without knowing it, or how to dance, one cannot just enter into grace, as if it were a simple contract. Grace is an achievement, like style, and it is an elite club; this is not to deny the internal feelings of grace, or flow, that one may have; grace is an attribute of a body, flow is a feeling within a body. Grace does come from an inner discipline, but it manifests only on the surface of our limbs and fingers. Graceful bodies are beautiful to look at.

Are all serious feats of strength graceful? No. Grace in bouldering has evolved because hard bouldering involves the secret ingredient of grace, its practical quality, residing no doubt next to its aesthetic quality. Efficiency is the alter ego of grace, though they are not in opposition; rather, pure efficiency is necessary to grace, i.e., no wasted movements. Grace tells of the body's low muscular pulse in difficult situations and given that most boulder problems involve more than one move, grace is another word for extremely efficient bouldering. That is – no waste while moving the body to the top of the problem. Ondra climbs the hardest in the world, not in spite of finding the most efficient beta, but because of it. Wasted movement adds up, and too much accumulation leads to failure. Grace is also soft movement: footwork like Fred Nicole, the precision of Marc Le Menestrel. It is the standardisation of efficiency, displaying itself to the spectator as the *superior* way.

One has not conquered anything with grace – one can never conquer movement, only reside *in it* with more awareness than others. To reside, however, requires training. I can pick up a tennis racket and hit the hell out of the ball, but the stroke is not engrained in my body as it would be for a pro. For me, a swing of the racket has no flow, no history – a wild swing tells me nothing, whereas, for a pro, a swing immediately relays a massive quantity of information (feedback). A golfer can tell immediately after striking the ball that they just hooked it; they don't even need to look. For elite athletes, the relay of bodily information is near-instantaneous. In order to develop this extreme pattern of sensitivity, a relation must be cultivated not unlike the unspoken language marking human relationships. As boulderers going for a dyno, we always know if we executed the move *before* getting close to the hold. Making the right move is not grace, but grace can only inhabit the body in which patterns of recognition are intentional, ingrained, and intelligent. The body requires history and memory to produce the aesthetic of grace. Eventually, your body will crave the emotions that grace produces.

It is not that bouldering requires grace, as we've all witnessed a few knee-scraping sends, but that the mastery of movement itself requires a particular appearance. This appearance is that of elegance to the spectator, but to the boulderer it is not about making difficult moves but rather about doing the *right* movement. This requires years of training and self-perception. Eventually, the body internalises this movement and finds great joy in the movement itself, masking the painful process it took to get there – in this sense it is an art, for art always involves illusion. All art wears a mask, said Nietzsche, and in our present case, the body is the mask that covers pain.

A boulder problem is difficult, but movement cannot be difficult. Movement just *is* – it is difficult only to a body taking part in it. Is it difficult for a ball to roll down a hill? Is it difficult for a leaf to fall from a tree? Movement is never right or wrong; movement never stops, ever. What makes a correct movement differ from an incorrect movement is how we utilise movement as a *means towards an end*. Movement becomes moralised, so to speak, when we give it a task. Applied movement, movement with telos (aim). Without an end, movement is aimless and ceaseless in itself.

TECHNOLOGIES V. TECHNOLOGY

Bouldering's closest link to the movement arts, and modernity as a whole, is this: bouldering is a *technology of the body*. When a body is unconscious in the hospital and is plugged up every which way to screens, tubes, and wires – these are technologies. Technologies support the body. Technologies are fleeting prosthetic devices for the body's survival, and they are indices of the body's ability to link up with things *other than itself*. Technologies discipline the body for the desired end (telos) and, at the same time, open it up. Technologies increase the body's capability to perform functions, to experience more and feel more.

The problem with theories of modernity, it's often argued, is that technology is the very thing disembodying us, the same thing taking our bodies away from us. The claim is that modern technologies allow the body to perform something it couldn't do naturally, making the body impure or somehow less human. We are cyborgs, philosopher Donna Haraway wrote in *A Cyborg Manifesto*, where the traditional boundaries of human/machine, mind/technology and inside/outside are blurred. Micro-processors installed in our minds will likely be standard fare in a decade or two, acting much like hearing devices do today, except the brain will benefit from externalized computing power.

Technology, however, is not just a 19th-century phenomenon. The *apparatus* in sports is the original technology. Its necessity for all things athletic (the ball, the stage, club, field, etc.) reveals how sport expands our bodies' potentiality. Technologies are indices of what a body can do, but they also reveal to us what it can't do – in this sense, they are items of utopian imaginations. Technologies mark the body at limit-experiences, experiences at which the body is threatened with disintegration (spacesuits or deep-sea-diving technology in situations where the body couldn't ordinarily survive), death (medicine), injury (prosthetics), or joy and moments of euphoria (drugs). In other words, limit-experiences require an *other-to-the-body*, something that is not it, but which can be attached to it in some manner.

Some technologies, such as steroids, surgeries, and other performance-enhancing processes, are more concrete than 'natural' or found technologies, such as bouldering. But in the end, the many types of technologies fold into the same idea. A technology can be intrusive and inhuman (chemicals), externalised but considered acceptable (a racket or a bike), or found and organic (the boulder problem). The aim is the same – enhancing the body's potentiality.

Contemporary technology is pushing the limits of what a body is and what it can do. For this reason, our age is often termed the 'post-human,' or cyborg, because there are numerous sectors in our culture trying to do just that – move beyond the human. It is happening in the military, medicine, and science, and it did not take long for the controversies that plagued the late 20th century in these areas to visit athletics. Controversies concerning fair play in sport make this apparent. Does the full-body swimsuit move one's flesh outwards towards space and constitute a 'body' other than one's own, as the recent disputes in swimming attest – a second flesh, as it were? What about the debate over sprinters with prosthetic, 'cheetah' legs? And what about steroids and PEDs?

The assumption that the body has definite limits, usually organic and almost always based on simple perceptual cues – the skin stops there – is beginning to be replaced with a notion that the body is an admixture, that is, the opposite of a closed entity. Contemporary societies believe the body is open, a montage of materials, chemicals, bacteria, and thoughts. The contemporary understanding of the body is that it is not a closed entity, but a *being-in-relation* and bouldering as a sport of 'relationality' could not have formed in any other cultural climate. Relation is, in fact, the *sine qua non* of bouldering.

Each hold, in its own way, is a technology with which we link up. Certain bodies require singular technologies. A singularity is that which is entirely original. With its emphasis on specific holds and the joy the body undergoes when pulling on those holds, boulder problems are singular technologies of the body. The so-called 'classic' boulder problem – one in which excellent movement combined with setting, rock quality and prominence – is a found technology in nature, almost akin to the found object in art. Font, Hueco, Bishop, Rocklands – these areas are famous because of their ability to produce classics at all grades since for every well-known area there are dozens that climbers just don't go to, or at least, areas that don't have the secret formula. The boulder problem, like the other apparatus in sports, colonises a certain aspect of the body that cannot be found otherwise.

A mythology of historical and geological purity inhabits the culture of bouldering and what counts as legit bouldering. Without question, many have climbed boulders blasted from the mountains, whether by road construction or some other process, and this is considered acceptable, though not always desirable. Yet it would feel strangely obscene, if not downright criminal, if a remote town, city, or county 'made' a boulder field in the hopes of increasing tourism. Or what is more likely if boulders were to be moved from the mountains to cities. The recent transportation of a giant boulder to an outdoor art gallery in Los Angeles comes to mind. Michael Heizer's 'Levitated Mass' is that stone. The boulder, weighing in at around 340 tons and costing 70,000 US dollars, was suspended over a trench through which visitors could walk underneath. This granite boulder would have more than a few boulder problems on it. With some nearby cliffs, some dynamite and some heavy lifting, any town in the future could create an outdoor boulder field. What would be the status of these boulders? What about buildering problems? They would surely be below the quality of a boulder in the gym since the latter has no pretence to be anything other than what it is. Already cities have contracted to have artificial boulders placed in their parks, quality boulders too, and, well, these boulders have eliminates and perma-chalk on the holds. When in Rome, as they say. We drive on roads paving miles of virgin forest and find it acceptable, but once we approach the boulder, it *ought* to sit there as nature dictates. Should it be blasted, the movement that is created feels cheap, artificial, something not dictated by wind, water, and sun. That the naturalness of our boulders comes to us without impurities is paramount, or, at least, that is the story we tell ourselves.

Jamie Emerson was right to bring up the notion of classic 'indoor' problems. We must have a platform-agnostic perspective of movement – that is, we must not get caught up with concepts like purity (outside) v. impurity (plastic). Movement cares little for the grand ideology of nature; when it climbs, the body doesn't know where it is and is largely blind to apparatus and landscape. Movement must always be judged for its own sake, not where it is occurring. Movement ought not to have 'place' or 'landscape' attached to it. And to those who claim that indoor movement is less of climbing than outdoor movement, it is like saying that when one runs in a stadium, one participates less in the essence of running than, say, wilderness running. The location of the act does not matter – all is a means to an end. The phenomenal growth of the 'board' in indoor gyms – the MoonBoard, Kilter Board, etc. – and the 'classics' that exist on them is a testament to a thirst for a shared set of aesthetic moves, able to be used by all. The inspiration behind the MoonBoard was to allow anyone to try out the problems on Sheffield's famous School Room boards, homemade walls made famous by Jerry Moffat and Ben Moon. Being able to repeat a classic Moffatt 8a from the late 1990s is like riding a bike that won the Tour De France in the same era – history and nostalgia are communicated. Soon, technology enabling gyms to copy World Cup problems on their home walls will be a thing, further eroding the decades-long obsession with purity.

A boulder problem tells us nothing about itself, nothing about the stone, only about our own bodies. We cannot know the true matter of granite aside from how it feels to our skin. When we take into account our skin type, body heat, finger construction and whatnot, we quickly learn that the rock is what our bodies make of it. The same thing goes for a body, as one cannot imagine what a body is without an externality with which it must be in contact.

A body exists only in relation to an Other, which is not to say that it doesn't exist, only that its properties are relational and that any claim to an ultimate property forgets that it is a conditioned mind making that claim. The only thing in bouldering we are privilege to is the *event* between rock and flesh, the latter involving our complete history. Bouldering is a third term between these two, a styled synthesis of parts we think we know – we think we know the rock and we think we know our bodies, and yet why is it that we succeed at bouldering only when we get to know the rock better – when we dive deeper into a relationship with it? We cannot know the rock as we know others. Rock does not change. Rock has no personality, but the nature of the rock is affected by conditions, such as humidity, which in turn alters the event of movement.

Because they increase the capacity of a body, technologies induce psychological states (affect). Distinguished from emotions, which are states of personal experience, affects are the forces of relationalities that can, in most cases, inform our emotions. Why so much joy in the dyno? Why do we sit in bed when we can't sleep and relive a particular move over and over again? Obsession maybe. The body tells us it enjoys even the difficult move because it gets better, not worse, at making the move the more it is repeated. It is the nature of a body to adapt when pressed, which is a rather pedestrian way of rephrasing the most basic fact of athletic training: intensity forces adaptation and adaptation translates to an increase in ability to undergo future intensity.

Bouldering would cease to exist if it were the body's habit forever to get worse after attempts, though we sometimes feel this is the case. A once-difficult latch, awkward and low percentage, can be done with complete grace in a few sessions. But this is beside the point right now. Our bodies are drawn to certain problems because they link us to something singular in our organism's physics. What brings us to bouldering may be competition and ego, but what brought our bodies and culture to bouldering is entirely different. Bouldering is popular today because it has provided an athletic experience that has yet to be provided by other sports.

⌘

WHERE DOES A BODY BEGIN?

A good education is usually harmful to a dancer.
A good calf is better than a good head.

Agnes de Mille

The reason it can take so long to complete a problem is because bouldering movements are very, very difficult to master. One does not master the body, nor the rock, but the third phenomenon in between: their interaction – the relation. Simply getting into and out of movements can be the crux of a problem. One is reminded of a horizontal compression move, as in *The Dagger* (V14/8b+) – two toe hooks, two hands for slopers, and it takes all one's might to hold this tension. One must keep the abs tensed, the tips of the toes taut and tight, arms and fingers pressing towards the toes but levering on the shoulder, and then, after setting up this position and dwelling in it for a while, one has constructed the necessary movement. But we are only passing *through* this movement, as there is no such thing as posture in climbing, such as a stopping of movement. We are always moving. In many ways, simply holding a crux position can be relatively easy, whereas having to move *to* it, and *through* it, is the hard part.

Our bodies are in constant flux. Change is our only constant, relationality our only friend. After this toe hook, we must find an exit. The way out will be different for each person, but it is a small cavity or weakness in the movement that presents itself intuitively to us, and we have to be in the position to feel it and escape through the exit offered by this movement; sometimes our escape is scripted, other times spontaneous. We have to be creative since things change, and we all, for some reason or another, change our beta mid-route for no good reason, forcing a recalibration. At other times, we can do moves so well that we become stuck in them and can't move. Sometimes we can escape the extreme tension with a foot wiggle or the releasing of a finger, but the 'static' energy of the compression must now give way to active movement. Resonating through the body, the subtle shifts in energy are recorded, the slate wiped clean, and we must now respond to an entirely different culture of movement.

⌘

What about the idea that bouldering is pure? Why should a piece of gear or a rope alter the movement-experience in such a way as to render it more contrived or more superficial? The easy answer, one which we have heard a lot, is that bouldering is pure movement, movement unencumbered by the trappings of technology and safety. Pure freedom. Gear forces us to stop. We stop in mid-Gaston to clip or place a stopper, and so what *was* happening – the body's flight from one hold to the next – is interrupted by an alien intrusion. Our body's consciousness of movement was made to cater to something that essentially didn't belong to it. We exited the mystical space of movement, had to account for the body's safety via protection, and then enter movement again, if only till we must make another clip or place another cam.

Bouldering, in contrast, removes all these in favour of 'pure' movement. Bouldering is without props. Technically, the only thing that stops a boulderer (or that robs them of their movement) is the summit. Dancers, who don't need any props, could accuse boulderers of the same arrogance we attribute to other types of climbing – the necessity of something other than the body (what I will call an *alter-body* in some places: a body – of stone – other than ourselves that aids in actualising secret potentialities of or within our body). However, one could approach the problem more creatively. Rather than find the fault lines in the pure/impure movement discourse, we'd do better to ask the question in terms of the body. As I've been saying, movement is what bodies do. It is not something that we have to enter, nor is it special. In theory, climbing a ladder should be as joyful as doing Hueco's *Mushroom Roof* or Stanage's *Brad Pitt*. Cars 'move' in the same sense of 'movement' as elephants move. The javelin is as much movement as curling, technically speaking, though distinctions must be made as to what type of movement – when in the exercise it took place, and so on. It is really *the body* we are speaking of when we make this pure/impure distinction.

Where exactly does a body begin? Most of us will answer – *with the skin*. But as the largest organ on the body, the skin ceaselessly dedicates itself to *opening up* the body as much as closing it down. Skin is not so much an umbrella as a passage, a membrane, at once functioning to protect but also to inform. Skin is relation, and bouldering is unique in that it is a sport about skin – skin temperatures, friction, smooth skin, cut skin, skin health, pink tips, graded tips, split tips, palm-size slopers, etc. When climbing at the limit, skin is essential. Not just that we have good skin, but that the holds feel 'right'; the friction is top. The slightest sense that things are 'off' on your skin is enough reason to pause. Ondra will even bring a portable device for temperature and humidity and only try hard when the conditions align. He's not wrong to do so.

Rubber is another form of skin, a technology, like a hearing aid for the feet. Rubber filters the information from the stone and allows our body to listen to it with greater ability – not *in general*, but with regard to gravity, for rubber on our feet makes the stone less painful and allows us to press upwards where required. One could certainly imagine a better material for the fingertips than the skin, like a micro-fabric for the fingertips to help with sharp crimps, akin to shoe rubber. And yet, as soon as we imagine this, alarm bells go off in our minds – cheating! Why? Because bouldering is an art of contact. In crack climbing, the use of rubberized or leather crack gloves has its proponents and its naysayers. For reasons you can imagine: the pure/impure debate. What climbers value is authenticity of touch. An art of feeling your way up. To remove this element would be to remove one of the great humanistic qualities in bouldering. On any given problem, we often sense an impending failure first in our fingertips – in our skin – before anywhere else; when that is removed, the game is changed.

⌘

SPORT OF TOUCH

I knew immediately when I 'had' the lightning-bolt hold on *Midnight Lightning* in Yosemite or the sloper on *Buckstone Dyno* in the Peak District. My hand, and more specifically, the skin on my hand, told me I had it. My skin was not slipping. It had friction – it just felt right. The hand, the skin, the arm, the body – all work in unison, and relation, for a send. But the skin is the last frontier, and here there is a lesson about the sport of bouldering. We have invented a sport where we must utilise our skin with an unfathomable intelligence and sensitivity. Our sport is essentially an investigation into the limits of the body at the boundary of the body (skin).

In an era of an increasing loss of human contact, we have decided to put a premium on an act that takes *contact* to its extreme. We have finally turned the body inside out and chosen the material surface of the body to express what is inside the body. As it turns out, contemporary architecture and art are equally obsessed with skins, fabrics, textures – all geared towards increasing the performative capacity of buildings, the opening up of the interior life of buildings to an external life. Are we not doing the same with our skin?

Sports are informed by trends in society and culture. Neil Lewis writes:

> Life has become automatic, as it no longer requires direct human actuation. In short, our modernity of ever-increasing choice and possibility may be nothing more than a masquerade of enslavement to commodity capitalism: 'the individual has become a mere cog'.

Of the climber's hand, Neil Lewis also writes:

> Not only is it the key tool of our dual self-definition as 'Homo faber' and 'Homo ludens', as creators of new worlds

and destroyers of old, and the means by which we sculpt thought, the hand is also perhaps the privileged discloser of our most intimate sensing of the world. Touch is
. . . the unmediated acquisition of embodied knowledge.

Sports of touch counteract the alienation of modernity and increasing mediations in modern life – in war, relationships, travel, television watching, reality TV, *Tik Tok,* porn. As a culture, we live increasingly more virtual lives, watch more TV, grow fatter, use our hands less. Our physical desires are met non-physically, we spend less time outside, and we treat the online experience as an actual social experience, which it is not. Sport is often an antidote to this malaise, this existential pain, and it is teaching us to navigate the world and experience it without the screen. The outdoor industry markets itself on this platform of unplugged immediacy with the outside, and, more specifically, bouldering, like roped climbing, is where we actually touch the outside. We pat and fidget with holds when we rest between attempts, hoping that this simple act of touching will reveal to us a better way to grip the hold.

For the boulderer, the hands and skin are by far the most important part of the body. We look at them obsessively, inspect them constantly throughout the day; hands are our health, and any injury to them is an injury to the entirety of our body, a liability, if you will, to climbing at our limit. Bouldering is a practical return to the mastery of our second most important sense: touch. It is a sport of resistance to the claims, and demands, of mediated life – of life lived *through a medium.* Through the hand, we access our 'knowledge' of the boulder, and we access our own strengths and weaknesses. Lewis continues: 'Unlike the feet, wrapped in sticky rubber shoes, the climber's hands have an unmediated relationship with the natural world.' As we shall see later, unity with the natural world is so often claimed within climbing circles.

As a sport of touch, bouldering parallels the recent popularity of minimalist running in the USA and Europe, which is a technique of running with virtually no cushion in the shoe, except a thin rubber outsole. This lack of cushion, notably in the heel, shortens one's stride, forcing the habituated heel-striker out of their mould and into a midfoot or toe-strike. Like bouldering, minimalist running has an anti-modernist streak to it, promoting a 'back-to-the-earth' mentality. The runner feels the earth under their feet with increased sensitivity. According to minimalist proponents, this rehabilitates the knee, foot, and hip joints to do what they were designed to do – which was to run. One touches the earth with the minimalist shoe so that the body relearns to be a body.

Regardless of its integrity, minimalist running owes its popularity to its status as 'therapy' to the demands of modern life, a return to a pre-modern bodily harmony, and, most importantly, a more natural way to exploit the mechanics of our kinesiology. The premium on 'touch' for Apple's products would not be revolutionary were it not the case that touch, as a fundamental human element of relationality, was becoming extinct. Prior computing was directive – we struck the keys and saw the reaction on the screen before us. Now, our fingers slide, dab and pinch, and the tablet can be carried to the intimacy of the sofa or bed, no longer relegated to the desk. Since modern life alienated humanity through the machine (phones replaced conversation, cars replaced walking, plastics replaced organic materials, and so on), the 'new' machines of the future seek to erase their intrusion into life by becoming more and more embedded in the body, further erasing the technological/human distinction.

⌘

ARCHITECTURE

Contemporary architecture speaks of site-specific design, where the architect first consults the space before designing the building. This is opposed to designing a building in a studio in Los Angeles, then constructing that building on an empty lot in Moscow.

The idea behind site-specificity is that something is singular about the site – *something* in the soil or neighbourhood. A context, a knowledge, an idea – that the building must express, tap into. In sum, the solution, and a building is a solution, exists only when you work within the materiality of the site rather than in the abstract/theoretical space of the studio. The solution must not pre-exist the site.

Libeskind's Jewish Museum in Berlin is a notable example of this. The history of Berlin is not only personal and individual but urban-biographical – a matrix of repressed social thought. To bring healing outside of the solitary building and onto the street, Libeskind designed the planes, directions, and angles of the building literally to point outside the building towards the surrounding neighbourhoods. For instance, the abstract lines that shoot off the building from its edges and windows point to addresses of historical German and Jewish citizens. Libeskind's building takes the context not only as something to react to but also as something to construct. This *thing*, which is history and memory for Libeskind, exists beforehand, and the artist looks to it for inspiration and style. The building needs to express this mysterious thing, or else its organic placement is in jeopardy, and so, the genre of creativity becomes adaptive. It is aluminium-box architecture against which site-specificity is trying to rebel. For modernist architecture, if the model or solution pre-exists the site, then site-specificity challenges the nature of the creative act itself. The contemporary architect must dance with the given materials while having his hand on his own design – both fidelity and infidelity are required.

Dispatching hard problems in different areas requires the same amount of attentiveness and listening to specificity of site. One *constructs* success by inhabiting this site more effectively – learning to grab the holds specific to each area or how much friction its rock allows in certain temperatures, humidity, and so on.

UK climbing coach Dave MacLeod reiterates the importance of listening when he writes that movement is at first like a foreign language. The best way to improve is to listen very closely to your body over time. Adam Ondra talks about the 'language of chalk', namely, looking for clues on the stone as to how to hold a certain pinch, pocket or sloper. Listening is an entire-body affair, based on intuition. One must use all the senses and exploit a basic tenet of contemporary thought on the body – a body is being a body when it is open. John Hockey and Jacquelyn Collinson speak of the 'eye' of the boxer when trying to read his opponent: '. . . boxers must learn to see in the boxing ring, developing the specific *eye* that enables boxers to guess at opponents' likely moves by *reading* their eyes and also the positioning and orientation of shoulders, arms and hands.' A surfer needs to read the swells and interpret an incoming wave; likewise, a kayaker. An ice climber needs to read a pillar – five feet in the wrong direction might mean bad ice screws and zero protection.

Getting better at bouldering cannot be done without learning more types of movement, *seeing* what holds require, and training your body to feel comfortable in that movement. The experienced boulderer can look at beginner problems and not even have to think about how they should be climbed. The beta is just there, in the holds, and your body just feels it without having to think about it. A trained mountain runner can quickly scan a set of switchbacks and know with accuracy how fast, or slow, they need to run the incline. Reiterating MacLeod's analogy, those well versed in movement are those who have learned a second language and no longer need to translate that language into their first language. Bouldering areas are our fields where we test the body's capability to adapt and see.

Site-specificity requires an incredible amount of listening power. Camp 4 bouldering has very precise footwork that takes numerous sessions to master. Hueco's power climbing will eventually teach your arms to lever out and explode off edges, and Gritstone will try your patience in subtle body-position and friction. In a video showing his process (*Rivers and Tides*), contemporary artist Andy Goldsworthy fails for the fourth time to construct an egg-shaped sculpture out of shards of coastal rock, only to admit that it got taller the more he learned about how the rock behaved. Failure was not failure – it was an index of his understanding. The stone had properties and, as such, desired to be stacked and balanced in specific ways. This is bouldering – we succeed not to the point of overcoming the problem, or of mastering it, but of moving in a way that the rock has dictated beforehand, through the holds it offers: site-specificity.

Another related trend in contemporary architecture is 'materials first, design second'. In their book, *Atlas of Novel Tectonics*, Jesse Reiser and Nanako Umemoto claim that due to the incredible growth and innovation in building materials – synthetic plastics, metal alloys, hybrid materials, etc. – architects are first consulting the performative capabilities of a given material, *then* designing a building with those capabilities in mind. The Denver Art Museum can get away with radical cantilevers and eccentric shapes because of the exploitation of contemporary materials – light, tensile metals and what not – and the architects had to know the specific properties of those materials before the design process began.

The materiality of bouldering is our body or, more specifically, our skeleton, musculature, and tendons. Add two more fingers to the hand, and the sport is different, or add another thumb on the other side of the hand, or two big toes, and bouldering would be different again. If we had three legs and feet, then the problems we enjoy today would not be the same. Perhaps a ridiculous thought, but useful in uncovering just how much the singularities of human physiology constrain our movement (and its limitations). What is unique to bouldering is the continually shifting stage on which we perform, hence the importance of adaptive site-specificity.

While dance navigates a homogeneous space (a flat stage), bouldering's stage is heterogeneous (stone is composed of edges and features). With a heterogeneous material, we have to adapt as much as create. We must not alter the problem from its natural or found state. The challenge is not one of creating a work of art (the problem) but of mastering a pre-existing work of art and naming that performance. As in the composition of a performance, the creation of a final act or bouldering sequence is seldom linear. Author and climber Peter Beal writes: 'One of the attractions of bouldering is slowing the process of learning down and ironing out as many individual bumps in the road as possible before attempting to link the problem. Yet it is easy to forget that every attempt is an effort at getting mind and body to respond appropriately to the challenge before it and that the adaptation process is seldom linear.'

At stake here – as in the ideas of *materials first* and *site-specificity* – is what qualifies as a creative act. Our creative act is not linear – we cannot solve a problem without intimately knowing our materiality. We cannot just go from studio to street, from playbook to field. The contemporary culture of bouldering develops what can be done with what already exists, as opposed to the *creatio ex nihilo* approach on the abstract field/grid of the baseball diamond, football field, etc. (which has been the dominant mode of understanding the creative act in sport). This isn't to say that footballers or rugby players have nothing to navigate since they have to navigate nothing other than bodies like themselves.

There does exist a sense of essence and manifestation for field sports – grid first (essence), then populate that grid with bodies (manifestation). Bouldering and architecture share the same creative act that sees as its field a pre-existing, heterogeneous field – something that needs to be navigated as opposed to mastered. All talk of conquering a problem, or mountain, is ridiculous, as the mountains dictate how we must ascend, not the other way around. Bouldering begins with the sheer beauty of nature's manifestation and then seeks to attribute to it an essence – movement. This adaptive vision of boulderers is shared by architects, and it is but a part of a larger cultural understanding of materiality and the creative act.

I do not want to say that bouldering is a result of trends in architecture or that it has its origins exclusively in theoretical practice. What is of interest is the profound way in which bouldering – as an art of touch and relation – treats its field in a way that accords with contemporary understandings of materiality. Both are expressions of a shared culture, and in turn, inform that culture.

In philosophy, there has been a revolution in delineating the role of the material world in consciousness, gender, perception, etc. While it would be irresponsible to attempt to summarise these trends here, what is unmistakable is a shift in emphasis from the study of consciousness *in itself* to consciousness as *always already* implicated in the outside world. This is the philosophy of *phenomenology* as developed by Edmund Husserl and Maurice Merleau-Ponty, moving into the existentialism of Jean-Paul Sartre. Sartre writes in an early essay: 'The ego is neither formally nor materially *in* consciousness; it is outside, *in the world.*' In other words, the intricacies of the material world are coming to the forefront as appropriate fields of study for the origin of conscious life. One can see this shift in sensibility in terms of exploitation. If exploitation was an old model of how we understood our world – as a dead, lifeless substance from which minerals ought to be extracted – the new model is of enchanted materiality in which every forest is a living, intelligent ecosystem. Now, the world is in full colour, and its landscape is a place of immense experience, valued for its wildness and living complexity. This is by no means a discussion originating in the 20th century, but what makes it unique in our time is precisely how bouldering treats these products of the earth (boulders) as phenomena with profound lessons, speaking to us just as the wave speaks to the surfer. We have allowed them to *open* to our consciousness and our life. In return, we have given an inner life of their own to the boulders – and boulderers protect them as dearly as friends.

In what can be called athletic animism, boulders have become properly anthropomorphised (which is just a technical way of saying that they have been given human attributes), to the extent that when a boulderer sees a boulder, he feels himself moving on those holds, and not just in a simulated matter. Recent discoveries in brain science and the perception of works of art – the boulder is indeed a work of art for the boulderer – have revealed that when a perceiver views a contorted body on a canvas or via sculpture, the body undergoes somatic states similar to the body position that the painted figure undergoes. In other words, we can view a painted body about to be crushed by a building, and our brains induce this psychosomatic state even though there is, in fact, no real danger. It is quite reasonable to assume that the 'stoke' the surfer, skier or boulderer feels when viewing their art conjures up a joy not unlike the movement itself, a joy literally between our bodies and the stone. Of course, we'd all rather climb a problem than contemplate one. The remarkable fact is that this translation of emotion has occurred in rocks and that it speaks to us, with natural ease, in the language of movement.

⌘

MOVEMENT I

To discover new lines and new moves was always my
motivation without thinking of pushing the limits or
being a pioneer.

Fred Nicole

It doesn't take long to know what our body does *naturally*. I
can climb three grades harder on certain problems – slopers
– than on others, such as crimps. This ability comes naturally.
Since it is unlikely that anyone feels natural on all types of
movement, the biggest crux in bouldering is learning to
move in a way in which your body feels most uncomfortable,
since nearly all problems will have those moves your body
just doesn't feel right doing. We change beta. It doesn't feel
right. I'll high-step every time; I'll use a heel hook even
when unnecessary, and it will work. Bouldering at your
limit requires these minor bodily interrogations. Success
in bouldering, while based on improvements in strength,
cannot be had without the accumulative effect of these
bodily interrogations. The body must become plastic.

A term used to describe movements designed for one
body and not another – *morpho* – has made its way into
recent grade debates. The issue is this: boulder problems
will get harder because they will also get more specific
and subjective. That is, they are going to suit such and
such a body type, and so, therefore, objective grades will
be nearly impossible to assign. This 'fear' is compounded
because bouldering has become a global sport. It will attract
more and more idiosyncratic bodies who can exploit their
idiosyncrasies with strange movements that no one can
repeat. 'Morpho' is one area that will create the future's
hardest problems. Another is where boulders are so local
as to reward years of devoted work. This is how Nalle
Hukkataival created *Burden of Dreams* (V17/9a), his 2017

masterpiece that is likely the hardest boulder on the planet and also near his hometown. So, this is a second path to the future of 9a+ bouldering – pure dedication. And yet, there is a third path – transcending styles.

Methods, which are ways to overcome subjective styles, are positions or disciplines of the body, and climbing has not yet reached this level of specification, though Adam Ondra has route climbers considering speed as a strategy to overcome limitations in endurance. Japanese superstar Tomoa Narasaki represents the pinnacle of sharp, precise movements combined with a deadly degree of strength. Seb Bouin represents another method of movement. Jimmy Webb the same. Because the common bar for success does not exist for bouldering as it does for other sports (such as the clock), methods will be as singular as the bodies they inhabit. One's method of success will, in the end, be determined by how one works with the body, regardless of what method is used to get there.

Revolutions in bouldering movement often come in the form of figures. We are taught to move because we saw other bodies move that way – this is just how bodies work; this is their *avant-garde* property. Boxing would never be the same after Muhammad Ali taught everyone what footwork was really about. Sharma's movements are powerful, quick and without regret, and in *Masters of Stone III*, as arguably the first young phenomenon of climbing in the United States, Sharma bounced and swung his way up a pocketed roof on the California coast. Sharma taught a generation of boulderers, plastic and outdoor, that one foot on is more than necessary, that instinct is just as important as calculation. In France in the 1980s, Patrick Edlinger brought a grace to bouldering not seen till that point.

One problem with the 'morpho' thesis is that it devalues the body's ability to adapt to new movements creatively. Behind morpho is a subtle apocalyptic tone – one day, the world will be populated with incredibly hard boulder problems that only one or two people can do because of their reach, fingers, hip structure, or this or that. To say such a thing sells the body short. The body is more alike than different – the difference lies in movement, not the body. Plus, athletes have long had an advantage over other athletes in terms of terrain and feel. It is nothing new. Nadal was primarily a clay-court player, as he just knew how to play on clay, but it didn't take long before he could beat hard-court players on their own turf, and vice versa. Agassi had that killer forehand, and when players avoided giving him this shot, he learned to hit a backhand just as well. The best boulderers in the future will be valued as much for hard, one-off sends as for a diversity of hard problems of different styles. It is only a natural mechanism to determine superior athletics in an era where the grade scale is stuck, which it currently is. If bouldering is about movement, then the crown will go to the athlete who can feel most at home in a wider range of movement.

On the other hand, one day we may have divisions in our competitions. Modern boxing has roughly 17 weight divisions within a 100lb (45kg) range, from Mini Flyweight (up to and including 105lbs/48kg) to Heavyweight (200+lb/90.7kg+). We all know that a strong, tall person will succeed more often (over the course of ten problems, for example) than an equally strong, short person. Today, we have gender and age divisions, but as the sport grows and recruits a more diverse athlete, we may have to consider divisions. However, the point remains that certain configurations of athletic equipment, and the rules therein, advantage certain body types. Often to such a degree that issues of fair play need to be addressed. Thus far, in climbing, we haven't taken that step yet.

If someone asks you to put up your arms, as the police might, your palms naturally face in front of you. Pulling downwards, as when we use a campus board, is the most comfortable position for the tendons and muscles. The body wants to stay under the hands, square-up, and not deviate. The legs don't want to go too wide, nor too high, nor the torso become too torqued. The body doesn't want to go horizontal, and the chest wants to face the wall.

Natural movement is the movement of habit, of least injury and maximum efficiency. Age settles the violent contortions of childhood, just as more bouldering calms the frantic movements of beginners. Internal kinesiology guides these movements, telling us what causes the most friction or injury. We listen to these internal constrictions without thinking about them. The movements we do are channels carved by gravity, bone structure, the grooves of tendons, the capacities of ligaments, genetics, and adaptation. In sports, we yearn to overcome these constrictions.

Dance has *the step*, and it could be argued that the entirety of dance (the leap, the pirouette, etc.) is but a variation of the step. Dance notation begins with the body standing erect, with the feet turned slightly outwards. To record the movement on paper, one begins from here, and all movement is but a deviation from this static step. This stance is the 'ground' of dance-movement. The same could be said of climbing, that all our movement is but a variation of the pull-down movement: arms up, palms out, grip, pull down, etc.

Habitual moves that the body does are not special. The body does not remember them – habitual movement is not memorable. No one remembers how much fun it was bending their elbow to eat a bowl of cereal this morning. This is not because habitual moves are not important. The opposite is the case – they are the most important. Walking keeps the body alive, and lying on one's back, which is a form of movement, is perhaps more essential. Essential movement is survival.

It is the *inessential* that makes the memorable: movements that are decadent (and aesthetic) because they belong to the realm not required by survival. Sports are catalogues of the inessential, though historians of sport are correct to note its early kinship to warfare rituals, which must have felt essential to a culture's survival, given that soldiers could stay fit in the art of warfare by practising the art of sport. Like art, inessential movement is 'worthless'. But with the increasing commercialisation of athletics, it seems the opposite is the case. Discovering movement, as in a bouldering first ascent, is actually quite profitable (to oneself and one's sponsors).

One bath
After another –
how stupid.

Kobayashi Issa

Non-habitual movement, which is the breaking of this formal pattern, is the *sine qua non* in bouldering. It is, to reference the haiku by Issa, a way out of the daily boredom of walking, sitting, standing, walking. In general, sports work within this category, but not all require the violent positions that the boulderer must undergo.

Solutions to problems work within the non-habitual range of movement. In what is now an internet classic, the 'wizard of climbing' (a.k.a. Dave Graham) speaks of 'imaginary boxes' that one must get into in order to succeed; boxes which, one might add, take a long time to construct. Likewise, a golf swing has these imaginary lines, the swing itself being such a finicky thing that a professional golfer can 'lose' his swing for an entire year. Tiger Woods went through several swing coaches to get his back again (he was critiqued for this type of swing 'outsourcing'), and it was a sad day when he could be heard saying that he 'just wasn't playing well today' because of a glitch in his neutral position mechanics. Swinging from a place of instinct only to then sweat the minutiae of mechanics is like being stranded on a deserted island – one has suddenly been alienated from a 'place' once known intimately, and now, will do anything to rekindle the relationship. The calculating mind does indeed help in practising a swing or learning the moves on a problem, but it is a hindrance once it's game time and you need to perform. As boulderers, we all know how mechanical some movement feels and how instinctual other movements, often within the same problem. A quarterback loses his toss, a pitcher his fastball, a batter her swing, a hurdler her step – this is just the nature of athletics, and there is no formula: one must wait and experiment and hope. Body position and posture-in-movement remain as elusive as anything.

Bouldering heightens a quality of body-consciousness shared by all athletics, and it is called *proprioception* – non-visual knowledge of bodily awareness and posture. It is proprioception that provides the body with the awareness of where our limbs are in space, and it is essential for human survival. Therefore, like dance, bouldering has learned to take a requirement for human survival and make it into an art.

Usually, this type of awareness is pre-reflective (non-calculative or non-rational), as one doesn't have to think about how to walk, the body just walks, but as toddlers teach us, this was not always the case. To boulder is to turn that which allows us to live (and escape death) into an exercise of living more fully. The old maxim that reads – 'art has nothing to do with survival' – is perhaps relevant here.

Boulderers have to cultivate body awareness without the requisite visual cue. Of course, boulderers look to the hold they are going for, and they track their arm and hand, but that is only a small section of the required body necessary to make the move. Aside from the hand, the rest of the body must move to a precise form without us seeing it; for instance, our hips need to be low and right of centre, but we can't be thinking about that during a hard try. Clearly, there is a learning curve for bouldering proprioception since we do not get better at the movement *per se* but become more aware of our body in space. We move without as much conscious energy, which thereby frees up other energies that need our attention.

Graham imagines invisible lines cutting through the body, and the climbing body, constructed entirely of these lines, acts as an organic object on a three-dimensional graph. Except the graph keeps moving in time, and through time, and encounters difficulty. Not to mention that the lines ceaselessly shift, and no organic shape or body position ever stays the same. This is ceaseless apprenticeship at its finest. Rudolf Laban, the famed dance theorist, spoke of the *kinesphere* as a topographical space in which the lines of extension trace the dancer's movement across the floor. This could also be represented notationally, the kinesphere including shifts of weight, facial expression, quality of movement, speed, etc. What we might call 'dance beta'.

Sidepulls, Gastons, toe hooks, bicycles, high-steps, heel scums, underclings – all require non-habitual form. Just as dance does for the pirouette, *rond* or open turn, the singularity of the bouldering lexicon testifies to new forms of bodily expression.

⌘

MOVEMENT II

What felt kinaesthetic was what I liked to do.
Contorting into a yoga position on the rock just to get
up didn't appeal to me.

John Gill

Modern bouldering was made possible by extreme amounts
of bodily twisting to succeed. It was this comfort with the
uncomfortable (non-habitual or unnatural movement) that
allowed the sport to professionalise. In part, we have much
to thank technology. The old schoolers didn't have excellent
rubber on their shoes, or active heel rands, or split sole
construction, or targeted mid-soles; now there are shoes for
steep limestone that just don't work on granite, and there
are shoes for edging that couldn't be worn with reliability on
sandstone desert towers. Their boots didn't have climber-
friendly heels either, so forget hard mantels and double-digit
compression problems. These were moves they could not
envision because the technology was simply not available.

Similar technological innovations that revolutionised
sports are the fibreglass pole for pole vault, the Tartan track
for sprinting (a synthetic surface that produces much better
times and is good when wet), and, in 2008, better swimming
pool design that eliminates wave frequency, which creates
smoother water, less resistance and, effectively, the shattering
of world records. China was later accused of 'rigging' the
pool to create more drama – in terms of broken records –
for its Olympic Games. The list goes on, taking us to Eliud
Kipchoge's 2019 sub-two-hour marathon, which he ran in
Nike's *Vaporfly* shoe, though the record is unofficial because
he was 'technology doping'. According to critics, his shoes,
utilizing a high-tech, carbon fibre midsole, were said to have
functioned as a technology performance enhancer, which

they indeed did, given that studies have found runners pacing quicker in the Vaporflys than in their regular shoes.

Technology aside, most climbers in the 1970s and 1980s couldn't yet conceive the type of moves required today. Simple movements revolutionise certain sports, the best example being what the Fosbury flop achieved for the high jump. Overnight, high jumping was changed forever.

We can never know why some moves, or the attempts to do them, soak into the psyche of a populace, but this is precisely what happens. Movement is the expression of a set of coordinates between bodies, culture, and acceptability. The design of modern climbing shoes reveals how we are using our bodies. It was only around 2010 that a significant amount of shoes with rubber on the top of the shoes started to appear, allowing aggressive toe hooks. Now, a boulderer would be irresponsible not to have shoes with liberal amounts of toe rubber. There are already knee-scum products, palm-scum products, and many more will be sure to come; fans and humidity detection devices are becoming commonplace as well.

Nalle Hukkataival's 2010 problem *Ninja Skills* utilised a type of move rare in the climbing world, and it was a minor watershed moment. He was not the first to use it by any means, but it was perhaps one of the first hard modern problems to require an extremely unorthodox leg swing. Because of the position and quality of the holds, Nalle found another way to generate momentum off the holds other than the traditional leg or abdominal muscles. Unable to rock violently up and down or to and fro, Nalle generated momentum from below his hips, using his right leg as a pendulum that, on its upswing, propelled his body upwards. In this manner, the stability of his hands and fingers was kept intact, something that was necessary where any excessive movement on the poor holds would generate failure. This technique was famously applied to the

Air Star project in the Rocklands to no avail – that is, until Kilian Fischhuber found an equally odd position to unlock the move. Now, using a leg kick to generate momentum is found in just about every World Cup.

We are now seeing the remapping of the body in favour of the multiple uses of the body's limbs. One could think of the edge jump in ice skating, which generates force with the same type of technique – using a limb as a pendulum (fragmentation of the body) that in turn reacts back upon the whole body. Ideally, the body of the future and the problems of the future will not favour the arms, hands and back. Legs will be used as creatively as the hands. We will have to learn full-body dexterity, and so a particular body type will ultimately be desired in the future. This is a natural consequence in all athletics – as a sport progresses towards greater and greater complexity and difficulty, more and more of the body will be called upon to serve its turn and work as a whole. A new division of labour is essential to progression, and the exploration of the body's limbs is one of our last untapped resources. Fontainebleau crusher Charles Albert has taken barefoot climbing to a new level, establishing, and repeating Font 8c+ problems without shoes, a decision that is, technically speaking, exploring a 'new' resource by removing 'old' technology (shoes). In a recent video, Albert has even made it seem as if, on some routes, such as an undone sport project in Buoux – *Le Bombé Bleu* – leaving the shoes behind might just be the only way to do it. Unsurprisingly, your big toes do better in small pockets than climbing shoes ever could.

Technology is merely adapting to how we use our bodies and how we create new genres of movement. However, there will come a time when we will feel technology is overpowering the body; that it is creating a new hybrid-body that is more technological than organic. When this happens, as in most other fully developed sports, we will have to debate where the line of the body ends, and technology begins. In many sports, the line has already become too blurred for simple answers.

⌘

ENTROPY

Death is equivalent to maximum entropy, complete
dissipation of life's energies. Entropy is the movement a
life form can take from order to disorder, harmony to
disharmony, high vitality to low vitality, youthful states
to older ones.

Robin Murphy

When the philosopher and phenomenologist Martin
Heidegger writes that we 'dwell in language' or that 'poetry
dwells in thought', an analogous relation can be set up
between the time spent in movement on a problem. For a
bit, if only for a brilliant second, we dwell in a mysterious
thing called *movement-affect*.

'Movement' itself as a term is merely descriptive. Cars
move. Rivers move. But we are here trying to describe what
movement produces in the body, for there is no such thing
as mere objective, neutral movement in terms of the body.
Movement is generative. Movement produces energies in
the body. This is a phenomenon not of movement but of
the body *inside* movement, of movement-affect. Movement
produces – and movement is itself product and production.

But for all our language of violent movement – dynos,
catches, hucks, tosses, slaps – bouldering is a practice within
the generative power of stillness. One can understand
stillness in many ways. Dave MacLeod makes a keen
observation when he states that one thing which separates
bouldering from climbing is the time we spend in one area
and often in one 'garden' of boulders, as John Gill would
call them. In the autumn and spring of 2009–10, I spent
an extended time beneath a small, overhanging dihedral,
among lichen, moss, and dripping cracks. With leaves for a
carpet and a rock platform for viewing, and the occasional

partner for support, I was trying a one-move problem on the Nick Stoner boulder at Nine Corners in the Adirondacks. For days I'd try the single toss move with my left hand to a bad sloper. I could look at it for 15 minutes while I'd rest, and never once did the problem fail to keep my attention. Stillness, absolute stillness. Equal parts meditation, analysis, visualization.

MacLeod speaks of the details we come to know about our favourite problems, of that 'stupid but lovely sloper' that has somehow infiltrated the daily workings of our life. Often, I am completing the move in a subconscious state while reading for grad-school, only to have the idling imagery of a hand on a sloper surface rise to consciousness, and I laugh. Wow, that was nice, my body tells me. The fantasies of sticking a hold on my project enter my mind without warning.

If dreams are one form where the unconscious bubbles up to the surface of conscious life in the hopes of repairing this or that malfunction in our psychology, then a repetitive obsession with movement is likewise the body's attempt to solve the problem put forward. Perhaps the subconscious repetition aims to perfect the move rather than just repeating it; maybe this is why we can often immediately send a problem after a few days' absence, as though the body was secretly preparing itself.

I know what those holds on the boulder in New York feel like in any condition, at certain times of the day, in certain seasons, whether it is cloudy or sunny, windy, or humid. It is one organism colliding with another, giving birth to another organism: the problem. We know each other well. Certain forms of life will thrive in the shade, others in the sun, some in the bog, others in the talus and boulder fields.

Boulder problems, especially the harder they get, will become more condition-dependent, and in this sense, they become creations of those particular conditions.

Paul Robinson tells of how, when he was trying *Lucid Dreaming*, he had to experiment with certain conditions, eventually waking up before dawn to send the problem. In an interview for UKC's *The Lowdown* blog, Chris Sharma remarked that this fact had discouraged him from hard bouldering: 'The hardest problems today are either super-painful because the holds are so small, or really, really condition-dependent.' A difficult problem lies somewhere in the crossroads of environment, body, stone, and movement. Each informs its neighbour. A boulder problem at the higher echelons of the grade scale is an organic outgrowth of a specific set of bodily, environmental, and psychological coordinates.

We dwell in movement, ceaseless, uninterrupted movement. Part of accounting for bouldering movement is distinguishing how it can be a form of stasis rather than dynamism, which is to say, an active calm.

There is no such thing as silence when climbing, whether in its spiritual, bodily, or psychological sense. Absolute zero is the point we never reach. Racked with pain, stressed to its breaking point, the intense flow and serenity of the send result from a conscious aestheticization of movement rather than integral purity. One could also say movement's 'contrivance' because movement has no original in which another would be its copy or contrivance. Sorry, Plato. Do anything for long enough, and your body will take on the shape of that activity. The bouldering body is marked by the boulder. A body that sits for eight hours a day for years on end will forever be marked by the act of sitting. Because of iPhones, text neck is becoming a recognised condition, a condition, you guessed it, caused by repeated texting throughout the day. The body that throws the shot put will muscle according to the exertion that sport requires, as will the ring specialist in gymnastics. Rarely is a ring specialist also a floor specialist, as rings require upper body muscles that would hamper one's ability to be graceful on the floor. The swimmer's body is as distinct as that of the marathon runner. Every athlete carries around their strength as part of their body.

> The brain is the most important muscle for climbing.
>
> Wolfgang Güllich

The toes of a ballerina, after years of impact, recovery, pain and breaking-in, finally become dancing toes. Bouldering, and the body it creates, is no different. If there is ease or flow or zone to the send, it is entirely imaginary, like calm water hovering over deep, chaotic currents. The feeling of euphoric lightness is the end of a long series of decisions: dedication to bouldering, training, passion, sacrifice, etc. Lightness is an achievement, not a state to which one has returned.

As Gill has remarked, this lightness may be felt only a few times in one's life. Sure, we all feel light after a road trip, but lightness, as the mystics have described it, is as if the body has consumed a secret sensation. Lightness comes at the end, and it is, strictly speaking, a sensation without spatiotemporal coordinates. Gilles Deleuze wrote of a certain type of body that no longer functioned with organs (these were too structured and regulative), but a *body without organs* that was organised in such a way as to be able to capture certain energies. Energies are not emotions, nor feelings, nor products of rational thought, but they exist impersonally, just like sunlight. Organs structure the body and restrict the types of acts the body can do. Deleuze sought an unstructured body, untamed, unlimited. Much as they are now, future boulderers will continue to use feet like hands, hands like feet, toes like fingers, and so on. The body must continue to de-territorialise itself to open up new genres of movement. And further, each new movement opens up new bodily affect. Joys are like precious stones found in the soil of movement, and the more dedicated the archaeologist, the more precious the stone.

Bouldering is the cultivation of this 'body without organs'. That is, the body is put into specific postures that cannot but help capture certain energies. Bouldering is an art of capturing, and every body is the accumulation of captured energies. A body is defined by what it *can do*, never what it is.

We do not touch the stone. We are equally touched by it. Each touch is a *being-touched*. In bouldering, the body is given over to the touch of sensation. Michel Serres, in his *Philosophie des Corps Mêlés I* ('The Philosophy of Mingled Bodies'), writes of French artist Pierre Bonnard:

> In the same year, the 'Nude in the Bath' appears. I cannot say that I have seen this nude, I cannot claim to know it, I try to write that I know, that I am living what Bonnard attempted to do. Immersion reveals, close to the sensitive skin, close to the apparitions or impressions in which it is enveloped or bathed, a sort of membrane, a fine film which inserts itself, or comes into being, between the media or mixture and the male or female bather, a variety common to the feeling and the felt, a gossamer fabric which serves as their common edge, border or interface, a transitional film that separates and unites the imprinter and the imprinted, the printing and the printed, thin printed material: the bath reveals the veil.

The boulder unveils the body as itself a thin veil of sensation through its immersion. Two skins contact one another, and each comes alive in the process. The rock is not a canvas, painted by us. We are the canvas, painted by the rock. Something about athleticism harbours a secret masochism. Our body desires its own dismantling – to be seduced and opened.

Bouldering is not a sport where the body is awakened. The body is awake every day. But more to the point, the task is to account for the transition when we breathe out, breathe in, chalk up, rub our shoes, and begin. What exactly are we taking part *in*? Sports are experiments in the joy of the body in certain activities, and therefore sports are virtual catalogues of the joys found in movement.

⌘

IMPROV

Improvisation involves moments where one thinks in advance of what one is going to do, other moments where actions seem to move faster than they can be registered in full analytical consciousness of them, and still other moments where one thinks the idea of what is to come at exactly the same moment that one performs that idea. Still, both the changing of the course of things and the riding of that course through its course are mindful and bodyful. Rather than suppress any functions of mind, improvisation's bodily mindfulness summons up a kind of hyper-awareness of the relation between immediate action and overall shape, between that which is about to take place or is taking place and that which has and will take place.

Improvisation makes rigorous technical demands on the performer. It assumes an articulateness in the body through which the known and the unknown will find expression. It entails a vigilant porousness towards the unknown, a stance that can only be acquired through intensive practice . . . Improvisation does not, therefore, entail a silencing of the mind in order for the body to speak. Rather improvisation pivots both mind and body into a new apprehension of realities.

Susan Foster

Bruce Lee, in one of his last interviews in 1971 on the Pierre Berton Show, speaks of the 'natural-unnaturalness' of movement, a phrase which sounds contradictory but isn't. Lee is speaking of a combination of instinct and control. According to Lee, all martial art's knowledge is knowledge of bodily force, so what he is espousing is a logic from which any bodily knowledge must come from an interior.

At its simplest, combat is the art of expressing the human body. Expression, however, is not wild and untamed, and it doesn't come *naturally*. Lee states:

> Ultimately, martial art means honestly expressing yourself, and it is very difficult to do. In other words, you have to train yourself to express yourself. This is not free-style drawing in art class when you were a child, but free-style drawing after you have gone through years of art school. One could argue, as Picasso did, that art school smothers the original sparks of creativity that is a quality of all youth, which it does, but in athletics it is different. So yes, while the beginner boulderer is bouldering 'no less' than the elite, certain experiences are opened up for the elite that are not available to the beginner; of course, both feel a sense of joy, which ought never to leave any type of athlete, but it's just that the elite boulderer knows how to dwell with more success, and ease, in movement. They have got past the first date, which was a bit awkward, and can now spend their time on more meaningful discourse.

When it comes to expressing yourself honestly in movement, dishonest movement is not about lying to yourself but more about being unfaithful to your training, or letting the mind get in the way of the body wanting to speak for itself. When you punch, your whole body has to punch, with no regrets nor thought. And Klem Loskot writes in *Emotional Landscapes* about power and channelling energy: 'Power Addict – put your head in your shoulder.'

'Be like water,' says Lee: 'When water is in a cup, it becomes the cup.' The body becomes a whole body or fully expresses what a body can do when its energies are wholly tapped, when all its resources are called to a singular duty, when the body can enter a part and all its resources can be tapped for a singular move, when all the body's intelligence can be recruited for a single, all-important act. This does not mean we focus all of our conscious energies on a body part or a single move. Quite the opposite. Consciousness is the enemy of instinct – it stifles the spontaneity and freedom of a moving body. Rather, a body becomes whole – since all of it comes forward – when it enters a part, such as when the fingers dig into a crimp or when success or failure depends absolutely on how well you manage a tricky match move. Morphology – this details how the body must cater to movement in its surroundings without compromise. But what does this really mean?

Lee makes it explicit that he does not believe in styles – 'Style is a crystallisation' – and Lee feels that expression, which should remain free and automatic, is contaminated and repressed in style, which can harm a fighter if one is simply expecting a set pattern of moves. Style can weaken a fighter if he is on the attack, as it makes him predictable. What Lee is advocating, and which defines a good number of top-level climbers today, is the ability never to be defined by a type of climbing, but to be able to do it all equally: to crush the mantels in Font and the crimps in Bishop. These types of athletes will find sponsorship in the future because, let's face it, we are in the middle of a grade plateau, and the level of difficulty will only inch upwards from here on out, in both bouldering and sport climbing. It could be a decade before we see 5.16a or V18, or Font 9b, if at all, in which case climbers are going to have to define themselves differently. Gone are the days when a climber like Güllich pushes the level of difficulty four times, and of course, sponsorships will go to the most media savvy, which is unfortunately already the case.

For Lee, the best 'style' is to have no style, though one must remember that this type of free, spontaneous expression Lee is referring to must come as a result of its opposite. Severe discipline and the rigours of athletic training are needed to 'overcome' the body's natural tendency towards bad habits; it is not so much that we need to develop new habits, but rather unlearn old ones. Free expression is not born readymade in our bodies – it does not come from allowing the body to take over in sport, so to speak – but is acquired. This is precisely what athletic training is: the preparation of the body in such a fashion that when it comes to 'go' time, the body can act without needing recourse to training or a set model of skills. Effective training masks itself. An elite athlete hides their training like a good paint job on an old Buick. Kilian Jornet was a natural, right? He may have been, but he was also one of the most trained, disciplined mountain athletes to step into the ring. Adam Ondra, a natural? Yes, but also one of the best-trained and researched climbers to have lived.

To be an excellent boulderer, one must work through all the displeasure of moves that feel unnatural (moves that are not one's style). One must train the body to travel with ease, joy, and efficiency, such that next time the move is encountered, the body greets it like an old friend. Moreover, one cannot deny how much the residue of uncomfortable moves builds up in our bodies during a send. They seem to gel together, and once a threshold is achieved, failure is inevitable, not to mention frustration and mental fatigue. Moves that are not one's style are like high cards in a gin rummy game – you shouldn't have too many if you want to do well.

⌘

ORGANIZED DESPAIR

Yet while style is the aesthetic of the body, and comes at no cost to the spectator, often it is detrimental to the boulderer trying to remain eternally open to new genres of movement, which must always be the goal for any athlete, regardless of whether they are taking part in the most 'formulaic' of sports, such as javelin or ski-jumping. The idea is akin to the adage for music: never make friends with a note, or it will show up everywhere, and you will never be able to shake it. Bruce Lee's posthumously published book *Tao of Jeet Kune Do*, which encapsulated the artist's deepest thoughts on martial arts, begins with a sweeping criticism of the harm that style – what goes under the heading of 'Organised Despair' – has on one's training. Style in bouldering is idiosyncratic and hard to define, as it lives inside all of us. It is defined by a way of moving that suits us, feels easy to us, and so we seek out certain problems because we climb hard in this genre, but, of course, the danger is that we only excel in this type of climbing and we develop mental blocks about others.

One could object outright: 'The boulderer is not in the business of practising forms. If we ever practise a form or sequence, it is for one problem only, and then we are onto another one. We are not susceptible to style.' It is a valid objection, but it does not address the spirit of Lee's philosophy. What Lee is advocating is complete fluidity of the body that attempts to erase all ruts that might have developed during training. What he is saying by default is that it is natural for the body to develop ruts and comfort zones that we inhabit but that such zones are destructive for the body's ultimate vision for itself. We curtail our ability for expression. This eventually makes its way into our training, then into training methods as a whole. Lee writes:

> When you get down to it, real combat is not fixed and is very much 'alive'. The fancy mess (a form of paralysis) solidifies and conditions what was once fluid, and when you look at it realistically, it is nothing but a blind devotion to the systematic uselessness of practising routines or stunts that lead nowhere.

Training styles, essentially patterned movement, makes dead what is alive, paralysing our ability to adapt through instinctiveness and fluidity. Contemporary, mixed martial arts fighting has, in many ways, brought this philosophy to fruition, since, with the erasure of most traditional (boxing) rules, fighters now face a more fluid and unpredictable environment in the cage, which means they have to be skilled in a diverse range of martial art styles: Judo, Greco-Roman wrestling, boxing, Thai boxing, Aikido, etc.

Lee expresses a metaphysics of the athletic body that drifts seamlessly into Eastern philosophy's penchant for universal energies. One thinks of *Chi* energy (read *Prana*), which can be found in Chinese medicine, architectural design, tantra and martial arts, to name but a few. According to these philosophies, this force predates our bodies, coming as it does from a cosmic origin, and it will postdate us. Chi sustains the human body as well as the cosmos. But Chi manifests itself differently in each form, and the singularity of every human body is marked by a different fingerprint of Chi. The purpose of cultivating Chi is not to cultivate it once and for all but to be ceaselessly in communication with it.

When Lee writes that 'when there is freedom from mechanical conditioning, there is simplicity. Life is a relationship to the whole . . .', he is drawing on the notion that Chi exists in a simple state that is both active and reactive force and that simply letting Chi be Chi is equivalent to the death of the self. It is the self that is constantly getting in the way. Hence: 'the consciousness of self is the greatest hindrance to the proper execution of all physical action.' Bound to the plasticity of Chi movement, one paradoxically attains ultimate freedom, because it is all too easy to slip into the habit of mechanical conditioning (style).

Immanent to all things – bodies, rocks, and plants alike – Chi energy does not just flow in all things regardless. Chi can be blocked, rerouted, leaked, released, deteriorated, and stored – it is a cosmic energy from which we draw. Lee's ideas describe a constant circulation of the body's energies to better communicate with the outside. In Lee's case, the 'outside' is the enemy fighter. Adapted to our present case, our 'outside' is the type of movement the boulder presents to us. The boulder and us – this is a very concrete relation. This is our 'unfixed' combat. This is where movement happens.

Though Lee is using the concept of style in a more defined sense than we have yet used, there is, in fact, no distinction between a becoming-beautiful of the body in the form of modern grace (such as a snowboarder's style or the art of our sport) and the sense of style used to denote martial arts regimens (Lee's usage). Each mode of style, whether that of a boulderer's style or a specific method in aikido, restricts movement unnaturally. It attempts to corral it, in the first instance for that feeling of grace, and in the second, to defend oneself. Lee advocates for instinct and the quick reading of solutions so that we are not pushing our perceptions (forever informed by our body) onto a piece of stone that simply cannot accept the solution we have for it. This is a process that, we all know, leads inevitably to frustration, excuses, and frequent failure.

Let's borrow an idea from communication theory to expand this point. A fantastic concept is the relay that must exist between stone and body in the course of navigating bodily movement, which we call *feedback*. Embedded in this term is the notion that the communication pathway must be unobstructed, open, freely allowing feedback between the mind and the stone (this foot would be better than that one, etc.). The more blockages you have, the worse you climb.

There is much more to bouldering than simple repetition and sustaining uncomfortable positions. Training your mind to get both into *and* out of the way is just as necessary, and the nervous system is in charge of those tasks.

As regards the nervous system, the story of Bob Beamon is unparalleled. In a 1970 article for the *Olympic Review*, put out by the International Olympic Committee, Ernst Jokl wrote the following on Bob Beamon's winning long jump at the 1968 Mexico City Olympic Games, when he beat the existing record by almost 2ft:

> That Beamon's 8.9m (29ft 2.5in) jump will be repeated in the lifetime of the present generation is unlikely. It is impossible that it will ever be improved by the same margin by which it improved the world record on October 18th, 1968. A jump of 9.46m (31ft 0.5in) is beyond the range of the physiological potentialities of man.

Jokl cites as proof that between 1935 and 1968, the increase in the record went up by only around 8in (20cm). Beamon not only increased the record, but he also jumped 2ft (60cm) past the existing record in a single night. Astonishingly, during the elimination rounds, Beamon jumped a mere 26ft 10in (8.19m), and after the 1968 Olympics, Beamon never jumped over 26ft 11¾in (8.22m). Beamon's record was not beaten until Mike Powell jumped 29ft 4in (8.95m) in 1991, about 23 years later, and no one to this day other than Powell has officially beaten Beamon's record.

Jokl cites numerous reasons for Beamon's success, including his race (Beamon was black). Jokl cites weather and wind, as well, but nothing unlocks the mystery of the power of the jump. But towards the end of the article, he mentions something more mysterious. According to Jokl, because Beamon was a younger athlete, he wasn't as formulaic in his run-up to the line as other, more mature, athletes. In essence, while veterans were busying their mind with counting the right steps, pace, and timing, which limited motor function capacity and brought more cognitive power into the equation, Beamon simply went for it, full throttle. He allowed his motor system to focus on two tasks that were essentially one task: run fast as hell and jump as far as possible. Beamon had no internal contradiction holding him back, no overly calculative mind – he was not simultaneously trying to control the precision of his lead-up steps to just the right spot while attempting to run at a full sprint. According to Jokl, it was this 'irreconcilable' tension – the body wants to run, the mind says to run a certain way – that held the other jumpers back. This is approximate to Lee's criticism of style and form. Jokl is fumbling around in the dark for a reason for the young athlete's amazing success, but what he is pointing to is what some call 'cerebral inhibition'.

Though cerebral inhibition is understudied in athletics, we all know what it means to overthink when trying to do something best left to the body. Grunt, don't analyse, is the name of the game. Nike's catchphrase *'Just do it!'* could be right about something.

The analogy to bouldering is obvious – ours is a sport defined by minutely detailed beta, regulated no doubt by higher cerebral capacities. However, it also requires an absolute and reckless contraction of muscular power, which is as much in conflict with ritualised beta as the long jumper's dilemma. As boulderers, we always need to get the beta right and at the same time explode like a cannon. The bouldering body has forever inherited this contradiction.

Following Freud's concept of how we come to naturalise external authority into conscious morality (the development of the super-ego), one could call the naturalisation of a bouldering sequence a process of internalisation. But it takes time. The sequence that at first feels awkward and alien is eventually internalised to become second nature and quite comfortable. After a while, a 100m sprinter does not have to 'think' to raise his head after the first 30 or so metres, or to swing his arms with an open palm, or to take the right amount of steps. Usain Bolt uses an average of 41 steps, and his body is trained in such a way that he will take 41 steps in nearly every race. With enough training, the athlete has internalised this movement.

As an ultimate task, the deeper we internalise the training of a sequence into our *bodily unconscious*, the more space we can devote to letting a trained body be a performative body because it is in the performative body where the real potential is. When we train, our strength capabilities might only increase by single percentage points after a session. Its influence on performance can be minimal; however, it is in the act of athletic performance where the vast majority can grow as athletes.

In 2009, in the wake of a mauling of a Connecticut woman by a 200lb (91kg) chimp, Alan Walker published a paper that could possibly be translated as *Why in the Hell are Apes so Much Damn Stronger than Humans?*

Apes, it turns out, have less grey matter in their spinal cord than humans. Given that this grey matter contains lots of motor neurons, which connect the muscle fibres that regulate muscular locomotion, it follows that humans have more muscle control. Evidence of this increased control can be seen in our ability to perform fine motor skills, such as threading a needle, or for that matter shooting drugs with one. The increased amount of motor neurons means that, in essence, we fire fewer muscle fibres upon request than our hairy ancestors. As one journalist aptly said, using a muscle for a chimp is an all-or-nothing proposition.

Walker cites a study by John Bauman in which young, fit football players were pitted against a male chimp. The strongest male student could pull a max of 210lb (95kg) with one hand, while the chimp pulled an astonishing 847lb (384kg) with one hand, under the pressure of 'when they felt like it'. This could translate back into cerebral inhibition and a theory – the mind doesn't just get in the way of blocking our focus (which is needed for athletics) but fails to engage the entirety of muscle fibres. This blockage does serve a purpose, for it protects the muscular system from contracting all at once, which keeps muscle fibres from being damaged. Cerebral inhibition, wide sweeping as it is, is also spoken of in the same breath as LSD (a drug that inhibits the brain's screening capacities), meditation (the calming of our overactive conscious system) and hypnotism (letting the unconscious speak for itself).

Humans, however, often overcome this strength deficit caused by inhibition through muscle memory. Equally enigmatic, it is still up for scientific debate as to what muscle memory really is. Some propose the capillary bed solution, the role of muscle cell nuclei, or enzyme concentration, or DNA-containing nuclei. Regardless, it is much more complicated than simply building muscle for a move and feeling stronger two days later. Neural pathways, muscle cells and many other factors come into play.

Beginning any new exercise, the body has to learn how to stimulate the right muscle fibres. After repetitions of this exercise, it learns to recruit more fibres, so repeating the move eventually leads to more efficiency. This recruitment capacity can even last over a long period of not doing that exercise, for one has already expanded the fibre range of contraction for a certain move and refined the neural pattern for firing to those muscle cells. And so, armed with this capacity that was not there for the initial attempt, one instantly feels stronger on the move months later. It explains why that hard undercling move sandbags your friends, who are much stronger, but who have never tried the move before. Whether we are more confident because we are stronger or stronger because we're more confident, we certainly do not have to use as much cognitive power on repeat ascents, for we *already know how to do it*. As for any trained athlete, the real problem is simply doing it for the first time.

⌘

SEEING THE FIELD

The entirety of the body must cater to each hold. The hold determines the body's position, and though movement can be forced onto the stone, it is only a minor victory. The same goes for alpine climbing and mountaineering – you can innovate here and there with technique, but only to a minor degree. The mountain has the final say, and likewise, stone tells us how to climb it.

As on a sports field, a change in position in the ball has an immediate effect on every square inch of the field. The defence drops with a change in possession; the offence immediately anticipates the gaps in the defence. Players look at other players differently; what were once bodies on the field that just needed to be monitored become threats with which one must contend. We see things with new eyes. The goalie, perhaps stretching, gets into position for an attack, knowing a certain centre-forward has a mean left foot; his heart rate increases, he yells, gazes, gains, or loses his confidence. Bodies are turned, voices rise, aggression morphs and takes on new bodies. This field has a living memory, what we could call an *immanent* memory. It is defined by speed and affect and the potentialities of bodies. The morphology is almost instantaneous, and the affect is palpable in the gestures of the players. Instantly, the memory of each player forces itself onto the behaviour of every other player, and these bodily memories – often vague: 'this guy is fast'; 'this guy cuts left if given a chance'; 'so and so will always prefer a high right shot' etc. – talk with each other. It is more than just knowing your team or opponents. It is about sensation, timing and attunement, and, often, it all must be internalized in the course of a game to win because opponents can adopt new strategies.

Our vision is like a spotlight. On a football field, we

constantly have to look at where we have just run from, as it were, to check that space for new developments. As an open field, space lends itself to being recoded repeatedly throughout a game, never the same way twice. The vision of the boulderer is akin to a spotlight desperately moving upwards. It is future-orientated; it can be past-oriented, but it shouldn't be, because even if we botch a move on a low sequence, we should not let this affect what lies ahead, though it unfortunately often does.

In athletics, the body is an open hinge that must navigate the past while preparing for the future. With the exception of highballs, the boulder below the bouldering body is insignificant since we are going for the top. This cannot be said for sport, alpine or other types of climbing that may on occasion require one to downclimb for safety reasons. As boulderers, we can be reckless since we almost always climb past sections that we could not downclimb otherwise. This is one aspect of the climbing experience that we don't have to 'think' about.

For all the formal training, play execution, and dribbling practice, a game has a fluidity without definable points. In fact, for many field sports, the mark of a good team is fluidity in transition, the ability *not* to require set plays; one thinks of the perennially excellent Brazilian football team. Always, the goal must be to begin to play from the specific coordinates that the position has given you. When a team needs to set up the play, the team is brought to consciousness, and such reflective capabilities need to be kept to a minimum to prevent thought from entering the game. We all know how painful it is to watch a team given entirely over to formulas, coaching, clock management, and the overprotective instinct of old coaches. In these cases of field and body, temporality (the passage of time) is measured in intensity and successful force. The latter refers to the goal, as it manifests the team's forces coming together to score, which is the goal itself. The clock in field sports is not just there to time the game but is the simple framing device to measure the performance. Many teams would, from numerous late-game surges, win games if only they were ten minutes longer, but that misses the point – the clock acts as an agent of intensity.

The clock is the measure of exertion. The various numbers found in sports, especially in track and field, are points where history has settled on various blocks of (acceptable) bodily exertion. Some are contrived, no doubt, but others are registers of what the body can do and for how long it can do it. Pushing the time of the 800m is not a fall in the clock, as we are in the habit of claiming – absolutely nothing changed in the clock. In fact, it is still ticking. The clock does not mark the passage of time but the excellence of performance. When an athlete shaves seconds off the clock, what is happening is that he or she is exerting more force over a given spatial area. He or she has mastered the field better than others. The clock only frames this.

The most important points in a good send are seldom the time spent on the holds, but how efficiently and with what amount of energy we spent getting to the holds. There is a rule in ice climbing that one should never settle for a pick that is less than 100 per cent. The logic is that if your axe feels less than 100, the next one will be worse, and the next of less quality, ad infinitum, until you deck. The same is often true in bouldering. I have never experienced such rhythms of panic and joy as I do during a hard send, a fluctuation of emotion that isn't ideal and not conducive to a steady mind, which is what you want. My foot pops, and my heart rips out of my chest. My feet sketch – how the fuck did that foothold just shrink, that sloper get greasy? Man, these conditions are horrible! I'm never going to do this thing! The negativity starts piling on. Hold your hand over a stove, Einstein once said, and you'll understand how time is relative.

On *Midnight Lightning*, the iconic V8 (7b+) in Yosemite's Camp 4, there is a gaze towards the bolt, then a toss – keeping your right toe on as long as possible – hand ready to grasp that first right hand, angled two-finger pocket, then a scramble to get the right toe on good . . . left hand up, right hand to an undercling . . . breathe . . . compose . . . pull your hips to your hands, smear the right foot on the sloper, oh shit, it's definitely going to blow . . . press down, reverse pinch left hand, extend the right hand, sometimes blindly. . . pray. One has navigated the field successfully and managed the body correctly. All done in perhaps 20 seconds, but what a *lightning* 20 seconds!

While there are set-up moves, we always negotiate them with the energy we have. Doing the mid-problem dyno from the stand is nothing like doing the same move four moves in. The boulderer must always be wary of thinking it is a send once they have made the crux move, as they have to navigate the move after others. That move often feels entirely different when you arrive with a different set of circumstances. This is, even more, the case with routes. Stefano Ghisolfi, when narrating his second ascent of *Change*, the world's first 5.15c, would say of an upper crux, 'For trying the route, I climbed this section a lot of times, but I had never arrived here so tired. The feelings were totally different and I felt it much harder than before.' In late 2020, Adam Ondra quickly dispatched the crux of *Perfecto Mundo*, a nails 5.15c (F9b+) in Spain, then battled for 15 days or so without a send, never really able to climb through the crux with enough energy to take it to the chains.

One must always have power in excess of the hardest move. Each move is a synthesis of the next. Each move is a summation of the previous moves' difficulty, and the first move is compounded into the body for each subsequent move. Later in the sequence, we always immanently feel the first move in the second, and the first and second in the third, and the first three in the fourth. *One always arrives with history*. This is true for emotional accumulation as well as muscular and physiological fatigue.

French philosopher Henri Bergson spoke about how matter and material organisms bring with them all of history. To make an animal, the world had to come together in a specific way. That animal is an expression of particular instances and materials – soil, sun, meat, water, geography, and so on. The animal carries with it all that came before it, and its life will add to those that come after it. Time is bound up like a knot in the fabric of its skin, as well as in our perception. The temporality of bouldering is a similar synthesis, where moves are synthesised by the body's ability to exert force. It cannot be argued that the body retains an equal level of force throughout a boulder problem. We are weaker on the second move than on the first. True, different muscles may not be utilised until the third move, making the muscles on this move feel fresh. It is the same case with triathlons –different muscle groups work in a planned order – one set of muscles is depleted while another is set to work.

When bouldering, the dominant trend of the body is exhaustion. Entropy, defined as the law that the body will grow more tired over time, separates us from machines. Managing fatigue *is* sports; excellence *is* successful management. The body does not fragment itself in retaining full energy in some parts when others are exhausted. The body is a whole organism – energy depleted in one area immanently echoes across its field, weakening the others. This need not be considered a sad state of affairs. Rather, this energy transfer can work both ways. Energy can flow in the opposite direction and rejuvenate the depleted areas. Though we may feel that we have more energy during the finishing moves when we send our project, this is not the case; even a kneebar rest can be inefficient and cause more harm than good if the kneebar is stressful. Adrenaline masks exhaustion, much as anger masks insecurity.

The human body is marked by fragmentary exertion. Only the Greek gods didn't have to rest. And it should be no surprise that the Olympics, and modern sport in general, stems from a Greek ideal of the athlete – one is in the process of becoming divine when one fights mortality and human fragility. To perform continually, without rest, without exhaustion, is a mark of divinity, as Jean-Pierre Vernant has stated in his depiction of the ancient gods. Humans need to eat, sleep, and replenish themselves. Such sputtering, in between great bursts of energy, is the trace of death in our bodies; entropy is not on our side. Humans seek out athletics because we seek the body's limit – athletics is where we go to conquer death or at least the trace of it. Therefore, depicting the gods in *athletic form* was the best way to describe what it might be like to be a god. It is in this sense that the human body is always weaker on the second move. We are not gods!

Bouldering contains another relationship to death, a less theoretical version. What is remarkable about bouldering is how, after years of doing it, we have 'overcome' all fear of death, most of it at least. Climbing is, for the general population, something dangerous. The majority of films depict climbing as death-defying. Take, for example, the American film *Deliverance*, where the hero inches his way up a large cliff, exchanging certain death from his pursuers for uncertain safety on the cliff. Now, I've had my fair share of 'death' moments in climbing, such as dropping a crucial set of nuts (which I was unwisely holding in my mouth) on the rope-cut section of the *Naked Edge* in Eldorado or being run out on a WI5/6 pillar with a horrible ice screw 30 feet below, but these moments are fleeting and rare. Yet in the movies, every third climbing move seems to be a death moment; see the opening scenes of Tom Cruise in *Mission Impossible II* to see what I mean. For most non-climbers, the central scene of *Free Solo* was Alex Honnold confronting death on the V7 crux. Death and climbing – it's hard to separate the two, often for good reason. The public imagination of climbing brings to our attention something that we, as climbers, have learned to manage. But just because it is managed does not mean it is completely suppressed.

The second pop-culture representation of climbing is the opposite of escape. This is forced entry, such as the *#stopthesteal* protests in America in January of 2021, where the dominant images making headlines were of rioters climbing the walls of the Capitol building. It was remarkable that these became iconic images, but understandable. Climbing and desperation, whether for entry or escape, is an ancient impulse – survival on both ends of the spectrum.

Death is not part of the bouldering experience unless one is into highballs. But watch beginner climbers get off the deck just a bit, and one realises that the act of bouldering puts the human body into a serious situation even when there is no real danger. It is almost as if the body is hardwired not to let go. One can see a beginner clutch for their life 3ft off the ground. Being able to hold on, which is basically what climbing is, is *living*. Not being able to hold on is *death*. The body reacts instinctively. At least, in the beginning, bouldering and panic go hand in hand. As if bouldering induces such a focus that the act itself – bouldering – becomes an act of self-preservation: our bodies instinctively associate 'letting go' with fatality. 'Letting go' is a learned art. Sadly, bouldering is lumped with extreme sports because it is associated with managing death. Wing-suit base jumping, big wave surfing, backcountry free-riding: all such sports can cheat death and allow the athlete to taste their mortality. Playing rugby or swinging a golf club does not put one automatically into the face of death, but there is something about bouldering that does.

As a sport with deep roots in the human psyche of living, escaping, and surviving, bouldering has allowed the energy of panic to morph into the energy of joy. And yet, here we encounter a strange paradox. Since bouldering is the cultivation of skills necessary for survival (proprioception), it is also the cultivation of skills completely unrelated to daily life (non-habitual movement). So we have embedded within bouldering movement the calling forth of energies related to primitive survival in tandem with energies related to superfluous expression, which have no functionality in life. This is not to say, however, that expression lacks meaning – quite the contrary. Bouldering is unique in that it calls forth these two types of energies simultaneously, blending them so that one cannot be isolated from the other.

⌘

OUVRIR, OR OPENING A PROBLEM

Interviewer: 'Describe your idea of a perfect boulder problem?'
John Sherman (laughs before answering):
'The Barbie twins are on top with, you know, a keg of Sierra Nevada. That's it man. I'd get up there and be motor-boatin' between those chop-housing jugs, beer bonging! Hell yeah!'

The French call a first ascent the *opening* of a boulder problem and say that the movement has been *realised*. In the UK and the USA, is *sent*, or more rarely, it is *solved*. But 'opened' is much more in the spirit.

What exactly is opened? The opening marks a relation between a body and the boulder. The 'opening' is closer to the opening night of a new dance that is performed – a singularity of a movement-sequence (a serialisation) across a surface. Opening is also a publication.

Opening a boulder problem is an invention; it is the anthropomorphism of textured surfaces; it is the personification of pure space with a minimal amount of features. Boulder problems express the rock for the boulderer, and the human body is expressed by the rock. Of course, for a geologist, or a miner, a rock expresses something entirely different – a geologist looks at a stone and sees past weather, floods, fires, volcanoes; for a miner, it means concrete, lime, coal, diamonds, something to be removed. For them, the rock has a history or confusion of minerals, which they seek to decode from *within* it. To others, stone means nothing – just stone.

Bouldering is a different process of hermeneutics. We don't open a problem by decoding the rock – this is not giving the rock enough agency. Rather, it *decodes us*. It makes us dance. We can try to interpret the moves, but if it's an undercling crux, we are underclinging. Fundamentally, it cracks our shell of movement – the habitual movement we used to approach the cliff – and renders this movement secondary to what it requires. We decode our movement up the stone; then we are decoded, then we return to habitual movement. Bouldering is a *passage*, like the work of art – a passage composed of a fabric of a body's spatiotemporal reality. We move in space, across time, as well as across space and in time. An 'opening', as the French say.

> We got by for a long time with an energetic conception of motion, where there's a point of contact, or we are the source of movement. Running, putting the shot, and so on: effort, resistance, with a starting point, a lever. But nowadays we see movement defined less and less in relation to a point of leverage. All the new sports – surfing, windsurfing, hang-gliding – take the form of an entering into an existing wave. There's no longer an origin as starting point, but a sort of putting into orbit. The key thing is how to get taken up in the motion of a big wave, a column of rising air, to 'get into something' instead of being the origin of an effort.

> Gilles Deleuze

As Deleuze observes above, some traditional sports effaced the origin of movement. But for some modern sports, bodies are put into orbit, rather than being the origin of motion. Surfers enter a wave already begun. The wave will crash regardless, whether a surfer has dropped in or not. Kayakers enter a flow. Though fields do not have such movement, there is an analogous concept of the 'wave' in bouldering, and it is geological time. Though the boulder does not move, as the wave does, nature moves and is recorded by its holds, textures, and features.

Deleuze is saying something about movement as well.

As a sport without a field and clock, bouldering refuses the time-and-space mentality of classical field sports. If one could define field sports by goals and strategies set entirely by human convention, bouldering exists because of a larger attunement to the *non-human*. It is non-human energies with which we seek to make contact. The type of movement that we step into, though seemingly generated and spearheaded by us, is intended to link us up with a type of movement that pre-exists and will post-exist the boulderer. However, when bouldering ceases to exist, our movement will exist virtually and in memory. Bouldering liberates movement, giving it form if only for a second, just as poetry releases the shackles of words or a flashlight illuminates a section of the ground then lays that section back to rest in the darkness. Bouldering also uniquely illuminates a quality of stone, if only for a second, in the same way that parkour makes active the passive space between rooftops and articulates gaps, distributing force over many points over a period of time. Contemporary sports colonise existing structures and express human attributes through this apparatus.

When defined in terms of the rock, boulder problems have beginnings and endings. But when defined by movement, there are no beginnings, nor endings, only alterations and the increase of intensity (on the body). We stand then squat to start, then pull onto the starting jug, and we think the problem begins when we leave the ground. But it doesn't. Capturing a boulder problem is like trying to tack Jello to the wall. Or it is like fencing off a few acres of the ocean and saying, look, here is the *real* ocean. We are constantly in flux. Movement is happening all the time, in all places, in all bodies, organic and inorganic. Movement is *life itself*, doing what life does, seeking to overcome itself, seeking new ways to thrive. Particles are forever shifting on the atomic and quantum level; energies constantly being traded. The problem here is rather what it is we are doing differently when we say we are bouldering.

How does movement change its form when we pull onto a starting hold?

The ground gets very little credit in the definition of a boulder problem, despite the 'top' setting the standard for what becomes a boulder problem. What makes our sport so unique is that it has two sets of 'ground'. The top is never really such in a boulder problem. Of course, there is a top – but this is not mountaineering. The goal is never just getting to the top of a boulder unless, of course, there is *only* one way. For most boulders, there are many ways to the top, but choosing the path of least resistance is not what it is about. I can hardly name a single boulder where the problem I am working is the only way up. Seldom does one top out, enjoy the views, have lunch, then go home. Rather, it is about navigating a series of movements, and it is nearly always *contrived*. Contrivance need not be a pejorative word but a fact of our sport. Again, the 100m distance is completely contrived, as is a Super-G downhill-skiing race or the golf course. All athletics and their fields are contrived, but better language is needed here. Sports are experiments of landscape and body, and apparatuses are the technologies of those experiments. They facilitate what we are seeking: namely to inhabit movement and to experience bouldering as emotional affect.

One begins on the ground – the ground is not the ground, however. It is a principle of movement. Off the ground is where the battle begins, but it is also where it ends. One immediately returns to the 'ground' when we top out, as though a powerful electrical charge has been dissolved in the earth. The goal of a successful boulder problem is simply never to touch the ground (the dab!). We strive to avoid it and what it stands for, to *abstract* from it, if only for a fleeting cluster of seconds. The ground inhabits the dark imagination of the boulderer, continually lurking in our athletic unconscious as the thing we don't want to touch, the thing of failure. Just the slightest touch can invalidate a hard send, as it should, for the same reason that track and field have parameters around legal wind, i.e., what they call 'assistance'. In uni-directional events, such as the 100m, long jump, triple jump, and others, a 'positive' wind (on the competitor's back) of 2m per second is the maximum allowable speed. Records broken at or under an event with a 2m speed are recorded and deemed official, while records broken with a wind speed over 2m are invalid.

A great word calls into attention the bouldering's strict temperance for assistance – the *dab*. One can get called out for the slightest infringement of brushing the ground simply because one is never supposed to inhabit the ground within our genre. The ground is the base on which boulder problems exist. In philosophy, to follow Immanuel Kant, one could call the ground the *a priori* of bouldering – the *a priori* is the condition of possibility of making a boulder problem. Without it, before we even begin to think of handholds and whatnot, we need a *concept* of the ground. A ground frames movement like a frame around a canvas – it tells us where the work of art begins and where it ends. The ground gives us parameters.

As we saw earlier, to be in a body is to become depleted over time. This is why the ancient Greeks thought our bodies ungod-like: that is, we have to rest and eat and sleep, unlike the gods for whom such bodily maintenance was unnecessary. The gods had muscle because it was symbolic of having no limit to their exertion; muscular frames symbolized power, beauty, endurance. We, however, are like a coiled spring without the natural tendency to spring. If you put a brick on top of a house, whether you come back in two days or ten years, the same energy it took to put it up there is stored in it and waiting to be released. Opening a boulder problem works in this fashion – bouldering movement is the boulder's stored energy from a bodily perspective. This is why the human body is expressed by a boulder problem. We translate the potential energy into bodily exertion that we have attributed to it, and the boulder problem is rewarded by receiving a name.

French philosopher Jacques Derrida made the following observation of the process of naming:

> The name: What does one call thus? What does one understand under the name of name? And what occurs when one gives a name? What does one give then? One does not offer a thing, one delivers nothing.

The name of a boulder problem is a subtle acknowledgement that we are bringing a new performance into the consciousness of human life (an opening, as the French say), that what we have done ought to be remembered and personified. The name calls forth memory, and the persona of the problem requires it to be named. One does not name the sequence of moves when one is in the shower. The great dribbling sequences of Pele or Maradona are not named, nor are Jonah Lumo's tries – though on occasion they are, as in Maradona's 'Hand of God' goal. One names children, pets, cars, rivers, countries, parts of the body. To name is to call into existence. To name is to admit a birth of sorts.

Colorado climber and writer Jamie Emerson says: 'If you've added new moves, then you have earned the right to add a new name.' Jamie is right to conceive a boulder problem in terms of movement rather than the use of specific holds, the presence of a top, or a strict sequence. Obviously, one cannot add a sit start on the *Naked Edge* (a classic multi-pitch trad route) and rename it; this is not what Emerson is advocating. Climbing is democratic because public consensus reigns supreme, and everything is liable to change regardless of the first ascent, including the starting hold, the sequence, the finish, etc. It all comes down to where public will and knowledge settle, and this is due no doubt to movement and figuring out the correct sequence within movement, being a public affair.

For all the talk of solitude and the boulderer adjusting to the stone, it is equally the case, and surprising, that movement in our sport is so public. We offer intimate and corrective beta to another boulderer, something a skateboarder would rarely offer to a competitor. Our movement is open to all in our crew. This is partly because the problem acts like a stage where one actor is performing at a time, then the movement is turned over towards another athlete. A sequence is a collaboration, and a solution is public, but it is always solved individually. The boulderer must take what they can from the public forum on beta, internalise it, learn to feel it, then express it individually for their send. But by the same token, we do give credit to someone for solving a piece of movement even if they didn't solve the original.

In general, what has enabled naming in bouldering and climbing is that our fields are not abstract but unique apparatuses with geographical existence. Maradona's movement in the 'Hand of God' goal belongs to him, not the field (since all fields are the same), whereas in bouldering, we attribute movement to the problem itself, which is why it is named. It is fixed into the landscape. So, to answer Derrida's question in terms of bouldering – 'The name: What does one call thus?' – the name is an acknowledgement that one has been called, that one had heard something. That something in bouldering is the joyous act that we think ought to be repeated, or 'spoken', by all.

The force exerted to begin, work out and finish a problem is equalled, in direct or near-direct proportion to the energy released – call it joy, power, affect – when one tops out. In a strict sense, opening a problem occurs every time we top out on a new boulder. An opening does not indicate that we have opened the boulder. Instead, it opens to us, and when we do, the arrow of time is shot backwards towards bodily memory and conceptual blockages; the past is carried forward. As the saying goes, you get back what you put in. The football goal, game-winning shot or 'latching the hold' (one thinks of Ondra deflating after clipping the chains on *Silence* or Ben Moon on the opening of the *Voyager Sit*) compresses not a future joy (because this joy is an attribute of memory) but the release of the energy it took to open it. Remarkably, after Beamon belatedly learned that he had just beaten the existing long jump record by 2ft, he had what scientists call a cataplectic seizure. He lost the ability to contract his muscles, and Beamon collapsed on the track, not simply overcome with joy but unable to stand. Though a full cataplectic seizure is rare, all boulderers witness or have experienced a sudden flush of stupor-ecstasy after an intense send, which probably explains why some exert a primal scream or others just sit down, apparently confused, unsure how to process what just happened.

Our high-key energy before a send is, for all accounts except for the boulder problem, socially destructive. We eat less, sleep less, daydream, talk less. It becomes anxiety in some instances, in others, panic of fear. We lose a lot of social life for the sake of this achievement. The opening is the beginning of bringing the body back down from its high, but we do not come down immediately. In the immediate, the release speaks more to the compressed nature of exerted energy, and this expression of the past enriches the future.

> To enter the ring near-naked and to risk one's life is to make of one's audience voyeurs of a kind: boxing is so intimate. It is to ease our sanity's consciousness into another, difficult to name.
>
> Joyce Carol Oates

We face the rock, and the rock faces us. We are in ceaseless conversation with it. When in the act, the boulderer's face is often hidden from view. To the spotter, however, the boulderer's back is his face; it is his muscles, tension and overall affect that tells of the struggle, the story. Her back tells us she is going to fall before her face. This secret intimacy of bouldering – the fact that we rarely face the crowd – will perhaps be changed in the future with what seems inevitable: transparent competition climbing walls; a demo plexiglass has already been used for show for speed climbers, and it was quite beautiful. If the trend takes, more a technological issue than anything, the bouldering body will be fully exploited by the camera.

Nudity is a natural consequence of climbing – we face the rock, open to the gaze of those watching us; it's quite voyeuristic, really. We all know those who never 'go for it' or those who drop before they fall; it is a most intimate affair, and one can learn all one needs to know about another by watching them boulder. We can discern if they are a fighter, or if they make good decisions, or if they are good under pressure. It is as if we are privy to another's most internal motivations by the very fact of their hiding.

Usually, the term 'face' stands for a blank wall without huge features. *To Bolt Or Not To Be* is a face. *Master's Wall* is a face. Perhaps it's gently overhanging or steep or a slab, but when we call it a face, it is unobstructed. Paradoxically, by calling it a face, we attribute to a surface of stone – regardless of its size – the very thing that cannot be blank on a human. The lack of a face is threatening, hence why, in response to threats of terrorism and lack of integration, the French government banned face coverings in 2010, claiming that covering one's face was antithetical to liberal societies. A face on a cliff is an anthropomorphism of the landscape.

Why has this term stuck? In this term, we can discover a truth of bouldering and our view of the boulder. Perhaps one reason is that our athletes, all of us, instinctively agree on an *interiority* to the boulder. We can say analogously that the human face reveals the interior life of a person. In classical philosophy, the face revealed the will of a person, intentions, feelings, passions, etc. The face was a special zone, the old faithful of the body's geology – the place where the dark interiority of the human mind bubbled to the surface and shot through the stiff flesh of materiality to be seen in the light, visible to all. The face of a boulder is likewise its expression.

The starting hold in bouldering is central to our sport and deserves special attention. Recent controversies over where a problem begins, how it begins, or where it *ought* to begin express a fundamental issue in our sport. As athletes professionalise and our 'events' (problems) become standardised, the 'beginning' becomes critical. Dai Koyamada's repeat of Graham's *The Story of Two Worlds*, in Cresciano, highlights the required fanaticism that *must* exist in any sport in terms of beginning their routines. At first, Dai refused to take credit for the long-awaited second ascent because he started with his left hand inches away from where Graham started, even though he was clearly strong enough to do Graham's method. Most people would call a controversy such as this ridiculous, and many did, but such is not the case in bouldering. Our sport, like all others, is a sport of inches and minutiae, and it does matter. More recently is the issue of kneebars. Should routes from the 1990s be done without knee pads and kneebars if you want to get full credit? Yes, of course. A kneebar found today in the crux of a 5.14d (F9a) done 20 years ago could easily climb two grades easier. The same argument can be applied to modern rubber and chalk and fans helping today's climbers – they are all aid. Sports do tolerate slight advances in technology as long as there doesn't seem to be a drastic and significant advantage. As with all things in climbing, the community should collectively decide what is or isn't an advantage.

Fontainebleau's *The Island* is another fine example. Where does the problem begin? Was Dave Graham's ascent the first true ascent? Bleausards fail to give Graham credit for the 'line', insisting that he began three moves into the problem, whereas Vincent Pochon's ascent, now called *The Big Island*, is the 'true' problem. What to do about these discrepancies?

Akin to the 'mount' in gymnastics, which begins a routine, the starting hold is a ritualised device for framing an athletic experience. All boulder problems have holds to start on, as it would technically be impossible otherwise. However, some have *starting holds* – killer jugs like Bishop's *Spectre*, Fontainebleau's *Karma*, or Britain's *Brad Pitt*. The classic problem will have a pleasing starting hold, evident to all, especially to the aesthetic eye. It ought to be pleasing to the hand and fingers as well. A perfect staring hold begins the perfect line. The starting hold is the portal into bouldering movement. Swimmers have their stands, designed over the years for maximum comfort and traction, as do sprinters. These contraptions are meant to ease the athlete into their event as smoothly as possible, and they should not strain the body. Track and field blocks (developed in the 1920s to replace digging holes in the track with trowels) were designed with the runner's knees in mind, the quad muscles' ability to generate strength, the angle of the body about to lunge forward, as well as for optimum speed and reaction time off the gate. If the blocks for the track and field sprinter are set too close for one athlete, the front quad may not be able to deploy its power, and if they are too far apart, the same may happen. This is why they are adjustable.

Golfers begin their hole with a flat plateau, which they will probably not find again on the course, and yet it will end on a similar plateau, decidedly not level. Soccer begins with the kick-off and basketball with the jump. Baseball pitchers start on the mound, and once the pitch begins, the play begins (yet one can still steal a base before the pitch).

Many sports have just the starting line, but, regardless, these mounting devices quarantine (or contrive) the space in which the athlete moves and in which play is confined. A starting hold is where we begin to create a 'fair start', a way to begin the performance without controversy. The supposed equality and universality of the starting hold are necessary for competition, the validation of repeats, etc. Aside from merely beginning a boulder problem, the importance of the starting hold expresses something fundamental about the athletic experience – that to enter it, a change in consciousness is needed. The starting hold is the manifestation that the body needs to be thrown into the violence of physical exertion. And sometimes, in addition to the mount, something more is needed to begin. Think of the gun start for sprinters or the bell for boxers. Something animal is awoken in the athlete when they begin with the gun. Rituals frame experience. They provide ease of transition and allow the athlete to enter into a bond with their event, enabling them to 'know' their routine, whatever it is. Anyone with a long-term project knows exactly how its starting holds feel, and the body waits for these cues before it commits to the problem. Moreover, we often create our own rituals before beginning. I used to climb with a guy in Colorado who would have to chalk up ten times, blowing just so on his fingertips between each chalk-up, before he could begin. If somehow he botched the first move, he'd have to perform the ritual all over again.

Derogative terms such as the 'pull start' or 'push start', or the perennial debate as to squatting on a sit start, are indicative of a failure to begin properly since the failure to establish the body on the starting hold invalidates not only the difficulty of the first move – because this can often be the hardest part of some problems – but the entire problem. With a pull start, one has not entered 'properly' into that specific movement. Professional American sprinters are now disqualified after *one* false start, just as a pull start on a hard opening move invalidates the entire problem.

At the other end of the spectrum is the dismount. The dismount, which is arguably the most important aspect of the gymnastic routine, is seldom that important for the boulder problem. Still, it ought to be perceived as the final gate that lands the body on the nether side of the athletic experience. However, there is a tendency to slow down and climb extremely carefully on the final moves of a hard problem, first, not to make a mistake and biff it, but second, to instinctively close out the performance with a feeling of mastery. A hard bouldering dismount, which also goes for routes, is called the 'heartbreaker' in the USA, or a 'gatekeeper', because, poised to grant or deny the climber access to their success, the final move dominates the character of a problem. It is hard to beat a problem with a dyno as its final move, as the catharsis felt on completing the dismount frames the experience, providing dramatic closure to an otherwise traditionally non-dramatic exit.

⌘

ABSTRACTION: ATHLETIC SURFACES

In art, abstraction is almost synonymous with non-representation. Modern art became 'modern' when it broke its bond to purely representational practices and began to take forms from life and abstract them. Impressionists took water and haystacks and turned them into fields of colour where the content of the painting became secondary to the *effects* of colour, sensation, and brush strokes. Cubists turned landscapes, forests, guitars, and bodies into geometrical shapes. Merely representing the world – such as scenes in daily life, cities, objects, popes, princes, or queens – went out of style around the 1870s.

Abstraction, however, is best understood as a verb – 'to abstract'. By creating an abstract object, of working from an abstract vision, an abstract field is created. To *abstract* – this is to take part in an activity with no 'concrete' relation to life, one that does not support it, glorify it, copy it, or take part in it. The abstract painters no longer copied life but worked with interior content – moods, joys, darkness, ethics, emotion.

To abstract is to remove and enrich, since abstract painters did not think they were veering from the world or avoiding it, but rather finding its essence, going beneath the surface. Whereas representation is fidelity to life – the eye looks, the hand records, etc. – to abstract is to perform movements where one's vision never leaves the canvas. In this manner, the movements of abstract painting are inessential to the daily workings of life, divorced from its cadence; gone are peasants, mountains, still lives. The abstract canvas, then, is a place of freedom, where movement is released from the obsession to represent. First and foremost, to abstract is an act of freedom.

Representational movement is a movement supporting life, what we earlier called *habitual* movement. Representational movement involves eating, walking, sex – these are movements ingrained in our bodies designed to support life: evolutionary movement. Such movements are tied to life because they allow life to copy itself and for DNA to replicate. They represent discernible and observational activities that one can recognise in an instant. Unless they are an alien, no one asks '*What in the hell is that person doing?*' when someone opens a door. We know exactly what they are doing, and it is not up for debate. To accomplish this, our perceptions work off microscopic sequences: walking towards the door, extending the hand towards the handle, pulling back on it, waiting for it to open, walking through the opening, letting go of the handle, etc. Take any one of these away, and it would seem strange, as, for example, if a person repeatedly tried to grab the glass of the door instead of the handle. Suddenly we'd notice that something is off.

Taken further, how can we describe exactly what the dancer on the stage is doing when she pirouettes, or spins, or leaps? Surely it is something meaningful, though she is not representing anything concrete. The movement is abstract, pulled away from habitual movement. Considered by many to be the mother of modern dance, Martha Graham abstracted movement from the common stock of ballet poses and performed some of the first abstract movements in dance history.

Like a canvas, the sporting field is a territory set apart for an abstract activity. Fields are spaces inscribed on the earth where bodies go to be captured by abstract movement. Part of the reason our movement is abstract is that we use an abstract surface. Some moves might seem more abstract than others, but when you look at it, all our bouldering movement is abstract. A sporting field, like an abstract canvas, is a space of movement divorced from daily life.

Just as temples and churches are places created by humans to abstract divine energy – where we go to sit, meditate, contemplate, pray and so on – the sporting field is an equal creation: a territory set apart from the rest of our modern landscape (car parks, malls, suburbs, motorways); where we go to be seduced by this thing called sport. But what field does bouldering use?

> Every block of stone has a statue inside it and it is the task
> of the sculptor to discover it.
>
> Micelangelo

Boulders are volumes on which we care little for the inside. All we care about is the surface. It does not matter if a boulder is empty, only that it has holds and can be climbed; the same goes for mountains – unless you are a geologist, climbers don't care why it is shaped the way it is, only that it is beautiful.

The Minimalist sculptures of the 1960s challenged the centuries-held view that the purpose of sculpture was to express a figure's soul. Classical and Renaissance sculptors created replicas of humans – the way our body looked on the outside was an expression of our internal state, the state of our soul. Likewise, classical sculpture had an invisible soul that outwardly was to be expressed by form, angles, and bodily limbs. Michelangelo went so far as to say that his job as a stone carver was merely to release the figure that was 'trapped' inside the stone, as the above quote indicates. This is but another, more classical, version of site-specific architecture spoken of earlier, where the architect works with a type of materiality with pre-existing qualities. But the Minimalists challenged this assumption of a body/soul dualism by creating sculptures that were empty and devoid of all human figuration – metal boxes open on two ends in such a way that the wind could blow through, angled sheets of tin, plastic circles, transparent cubes, etc. Minimalists were obsessed with surface, and it was a small revolution in an age-old art where the human body formerly took precedence. Minimalist sculpture had no 'soul', and that was the point. It was, as we might say today, post-human.

Boulderers share an analogous vision – we do not care for the interior of a boulder. However, we revolutionised this cultural and artistic obsession with surface by reversing the idea of interior/exterior. In other words, we have made the boulder's interior life – that through which it is named – depend on its surface qualities. The interior does not pre-exist the boulder. The life of the boulder problem, its interior, its singularity, is an *effect* of its exterior. The soul is an attribute of mere surface play.

So again, what defines our surface? First, it is populated with the potential for movement, in which no specific type of movement is ruled out. Only movement that succeeds is accepted for the send, and in this sense, the boulderer's battle is making movement more efficient and effective. Typical of an abstract surface, it can be 'read' or intuited only holistically. One does not isolate a hold and think they have the problem figured out without looking at the hold before and after it. Each part must be configured into the sequence. This is why the highest-quality problems are those in which every part/hold can be used, without exceptions. Only when the entire surface, or contained area, can be utilised is a boulder problem complete; only then is it 'framed', as it were. This is most likely because our creativity is never stifled by 'that edge is out' or 'that foot is for the problem to the left'; of course, there are contrivances, but contrivances are rarely considered classics, for these very reasons of exclusion. Formally speaking, a field is a field only if opportunities do not limit the athlete's vision. Hence the term 'field vision' to describe a superior player's sense of the entirety of the surface.

The Chinese characters for swimmer, deciphered, mean literally, 'one who knows the nature of water'.

Huston Smith

To echo the quote above, a boulderer (and climber) does not just mean one who boulders, but one who knows the nature of stone. Getting to know its *nature*, for the boulderer, is a process in which a boulderer must contemplate a problem since hard problems naturally require thinking. As a work of art needs contemplation to be solved, a boulder's surfaces, defined by marks and textures, need translation into bodily movements. Marks and textures are the holds. In his book on the foundation of Western painting, Julian Bell remarks that while marks are everywhere, only some marks deserve the title. For instance, scuffs on the floor are marks, but we would never consider the floor in our local café a work of fine art. What distinguishes a mark from a *mark* is the notion of causality, that is, intentionality. Bell writes:

A mark is whatever we see that we recognise as having a cause – whether that cause is intentional or not. We see it and we see past it, or into it; it is what it is *and* a reminder of something besides.

Just as medieval theologians considered God's existence as a clock implies a clockmaker, for Bell, a mark indicates a mark maker. A mark indicates not randomness (though it may have an accidental origin) but meaning-making. A mark indicates an attempt at communication. Bouldering is an enterprise in meaning-making through the interpretation of marks on a surface. A boulder problem is an abstract *idea* in the most general sense, as it is that which explains a series of marks. We approach and perceive boulder problems like the museumgoer, backing up and taking in the larger vision, inspecting the details, walking from side to side, etc. Ondra speaks of the 'language of chalk', or 'reading' a sequence

133

from the ground just by how previous climbers chalked the holds. On the one hand, the boulder problem means how it might be climbed, but on the other hand, what it could mean is a sense of touch desired by our cultural bodies. Boulderers at once recognise that boulders do not ask to be climbed, yet, in our minds, what else does a boulder desire other than to be climbed?

Directionality is an aspect of each part of our field, and the best climbers can tell from each foothold what position their body will need to assume to use it; it takes time, this hermeneutic skill. Abstract surfaces are dynamic, not static. Of course, the rock does not change shape, but it does when we are sending – sometimes it resists us; at other times, it feels easy. While the alterations are in our body, movement is a third item between the stone and body. The field does not pre-exist the sport *per se*. Rather, the sport defines the field, just as college fields are used for many different sports.

Sports are technologies of capture. The field is a technological zone with an inherent code (rules of the game) designed to allow its participants an optimal experience exceeding habitual movement. The field and the bodies form an integral relationship, unable to be easily separated. An abstract field almost always requires abstract movement.

Abstract surfaces are designed to produce emotions that representational surfaces cannot. A path or trail is not the same as an obstacle course. For an athlete, every field is a field of desire, sometimes even nostalgia, such as that which an ageing track runner has for the old track, the old rituals, the feel of grass, the stretching, and drills; or a gymnast when they grab the rings after all those years; or a boulderer when they imagine the shape of a hold on one of their old projects. What memory and longings are recalled, of a life that used to be!

The space of the field is a place of specific memory and identity. Something in the apparatus inhabits our body, and it is unforgettable. After a time, our desires inhabit this field fully. We come to wish for nothing more than merely to practise our sport. Fantasies interject themselves while we are at work, and we suddenly realize our mind has been climbing. We unconsciously grab the edges of everything. Buildings turn into routes. The Greeks had a word for an activity that was done for itself – '*autotelic*'. It is a word that defines doing something for no other reason than doing it. Bouldering is autotelic.

MYSTICISM AND ATHLETICS

Just as walking is controlled falling, bouldering is primarily the successful management of gravity, finding clever ways to navigate this downward force with the lesser force of the body.

When we say that climbing is a mystical place where our mind goes, such that it is no longer mind or no longer thinks – where it is in a state of Zen – we are only half right. Here, one can turn to religious discourse in mystical notions of effacement, dissolution and transcendence of the self or ego or *atman*. Nearly all religious systems talk of this process in some fashion.

Mountaineers have long spoken of a primal connection with nature while in the thin air. The birth of mountaineering coincided with Romanticism, which meant that mountaineering literature adopted a Romantic imagination. Such as being overtaken by the 'majesty' of nature, the mountains, of 'indescribable' feelings, the 'sublime', the ineffable, etc. Today, over two centuries after climbers first went up mountains for sport, Romantic imagination is alive and well in literature and culture. Soloists, not to mention the new breed of sponsored climber-extremists, exude similar language of being 'out of body' or 'in the zone'. Monks, Brahmans, gurus, priests, sages, medicine men – all these figures discuss this mysterious state. Robert Higgs and Michael Braswell have spoken of the athletic concept of 'flow' with the notion of the 'holy' in religion, arguing for considerable overlap in many areas. However, the problem with such studies remains that this zone, this mental space inhabited by athletes, is understood as a place of *unthought*.

Thought was mentioned previously, and in bouldering, we often hear of *the zone*, the place of non-thought. It has been compared (at least in language) to mystical states of complete bodily absorption – the completely aware present, the moment when we leave the world, and the ground falls out beneath us, as Klem Loskot and Dean Potter have described. But if you have ever been in a hospital and seen someone without thought, you'll have seen that it looks nothing like 'the zone'. Catatonic is properly thoughtless. I have non-thought experiences all the time, and they are quite boring. 'The zone' is not the ground of bodily/mental existence, which is to say, it is not something we come to when we get our minds out of the way. The opposite is the case – it is an achievement, which is why Susan Jackson and Mihaly Csikszentmihalyi, using a different name for this state, have written a book on how to achieve flow in athletics, in which they even argue that the purpose of athletics, and life in general, is to experience this state.

While these ideas may be useful for our climbing discourse, the language is imprecise. All that stuff may be true, but it doesn't do much to separate bouldering from a long hike in the woods. Not that it needs to be different. But it is. Bouldering is not a vista unto nature where the Self experiences its finitude – it is an intimate relationship with a tiny piece of geology. If one happens to have a similar experience upon a boulder as one does in the mountains, it is not because the same act got them there. The result may be the same, but not the means.

As a former gymnast, I would argue it is *not* true that the body is given over to anything mysterious during a routine. One is hyper-rational during a routine, but of course, we must understand it as a rationality of the body, the very thing we train for; the gymnast is hyper-aware in a bodily sense, intuitively, and not in a hyper-conscious sense. One can arrive in the zone only because one has trained long and hard to get there. A first-time runner will not feel the runner's high for the same reason.

I used to be really psyched on doing the hardest moves I can, but I don't know, something shifted in me a couple years ago, where, just being part of the landscape on a big beautiful line, for an instant, was what really got me psyched on climbing big, tall lines . . . for a moment you can actually be a part of that landscape on this feature.

Kevin Jorgenson

Kevin Jorgenson illustrates this nicely with some acute words in *Core*, Fryberger's 2010 film. Jorgenson speaks rather poetically of becoming the landscape in a manner that would make Walt Whitman, or William Blake, smile in their graves. Fryberger does not present just the product (the send), but the process, and it is in the latter that we can learn that this state of becoming the landscape, understood as the body's effacement in times of extreme measure, is such that body is so attuned to the stone that it is hard to tell (from the boulderer's perspective) where the rock begins and ends, or conversely, where the body begins and ends. Of course, it is still our body, and the rock is still the rock; the aesthetics remain the same, but we are here speaking of what movement does to the body, not just what it looks like from the ground. Fryberger shows how this timeless state of complete, 'reckless' abandon is a finely tuned, completely calculated, rehearsed and logical enterprise. It is as if all this preparatory work is needed to get what Jorgenson wants, much as Bruce Lee said of expression. In other words, this state, so often akin to the 'drunkenness' of the surfer's high, or the Zen of emptying the mind, is nothing of the sort. An on-sight free-solo or an on-sight on new rock may get closer to the surfer's opiate, but the high Jorgenson speaks of is specific to bouldering. The myth of the 'soul climber' suddenly thrust into a mythical confrontation between man and stone – who joyously rides an adrenaline rush to the top – does no justice to hard bouldering. On this account, Dean Potter and Dan Osman, or Dave Hatchett (via Eric Perlman), surf more than climb and need to be commended for doing so. But the myth has remained in bouldering and climbing, and for too long. One must train the body to transcend it – it is not automatic. The marathon monks of Japan, or the Shaolin monks of China, know well that there are specific entrance points to the body to exit it correctly. One must enter these points with rigorous practices to exploit the body's potential. One never 'forgets' the body – the opposite is the case. Whether one exits the body or inhabits it entirely – it is the same experience.

Boulderers speak of the boulder the way surfers speak of the wave. Here is a great quote about the wave from surf legend Dorian Paskowitz from the documentary *Surfwise*:

> A sea wave is like all other waves – an energy. From an energy source . . . the stars . . . the sun bakes down, and makes this hot and that cold, makes that powerful, giant star, over thousands of square miles, so in a way, that little wave has in it some of the wisdom of nature . . . of the universe . . . then you capture it.

Any act of surfing has embodied nature itself – the rhythm of the stars, gravity, tides, and sun. Each time you catch a wave, you traverse all these elements, allowing you to inhabit – however we conceive this habitation – the process that made the wave. A wave is never just a wave, but completion of an act of nature and a new beginning – a final act washing ashore only to repeat itself again and again. To say it is just an experience, that is, just *in the mind*, is to miss the very real and tangible elements that constitute surfing – the feeling of water, the sun, the thrill of sliding down the front of a giant moving waterfall, the rhythm of the sets. The surfer's body becomes, for those precious seconds, enslaved to inhuman rhythms of nature. A lot of surfers treat the water as just another field and surfing as just another sport, but that's like walking into the British Museum with dark sunglasses and music playing in your earbuds. Sure, you can do it, but you are missing out.

Boulders are also results of unknowable geological movements – water, ice, wind, gravity, heat, cleaving, splitting, falling, oxidation and so on. Holds may have been crafted thousands of years ago, and we are but meeting them here, in this short window when we find them. But the thing is, this history is never lost to us. Geological time is embedded in the movement itself, however mysteriously. It lives in the friction of the holds, the colour, texture, angles. We too feel this maturity of nature – this completion – in our movement, for when we move across the stone, we are adding to its geological history. We inhabit its life, and our human act is a *translation* of the rhythms of nature. To boulder is to establish a relationship with an impersonal event of nature. This habitation never leaves one the worse for it either. The lesson of surfing, like bouldering, has no object – no lesson one can quantify or teach or write down – yet it is therapeutic and medicinal for perhaps primitive, psychological reasons: the longing to connect with the earth.

Religious monastics have long sought to diminish the light that the body carried, attempting, of course, to dim it to such a point that they could get closer to God. They were even called 'athletes of God' by their peers in Egypt and Syria in the 4th, 5th, and 6th centuries. But in their experimentation, they made a serious discovery – by suppressing all things concerned with the body, they inhabited the body more profoundly. Paradoxically, to leave the body, one must know it completely, a process that leaves one in the end far too knowledgeable about the body ever to *leave* it. In contrast, this experience – Gill's 'lightness', or Loskot's 'groundlessness' – of transcending the self, so often quoted, written about, cited, and discussed in popular literature, is a profound *in-the-body* experience.

Such *clarity* is not the result of a mind/body split, but of *fully* being in a trained body, and it is one of the great experiences of athletes, which isn't to say it is something we always need to chase because you really can't. It often just arrives when it wants. It is unpredictable. A gift. Of course, there are some things you can do. Pre-visualisation is one method of digging such a trench into our psychosomatic complex to prepare ourselves for things we haven't done. When it comes time to execute these moves, we can then fully insert ourselves into this complex and inhabit that imaginary structure. It is as if the imagined world of visualisation (mind) and the actual world (body) has collapsed. What results is not a mind/body split but *an experience of the body* not often granted in our daily routines. In other words, the transcendence of the body is another name for the hyper-conscious body.

⌘

THE BOUT

Problems lie in wait. They sit there, sleep in the dark, talking back to us, goading us, frustrating us. Famous bouts circulate in the bouldering world just like the trio of Ali–Frazier fights in the boxing world: Dave Graham v. a repeat of Wood's *Hypnotized Minds;* Ondra v. *Silence;* Robinson v. *Lucid Dreaming;* Gill v. *The Thimble.* Nalle v. *Burden of Dreams.*

Just as any competitive athlete knows when they are in a match for an extended time, it is anyone's guess who will pull out victorious. Success seems out of one's control, and all an athlete can do is keep doing what they have been doing. Keep swinging the racket . . . don't fuck up . . . don't try anything fancy . . . stick to the course and try to have hope. Try to rest when possible. Tennis is a great sport to watch for battles, for it can go on for hours, even days in a few circumstances, and contest numerous match points. Each player has exhausted all their tricks, and each opponent knows how to defeat the other's tricks. During one great battle, such as John Isner v. Nicolas Mahut (Wimbledon, 2010), one does not know what they are waiting for – luck, perhaps. It could be over at any time, with any swing, but no, it keeps going. Each opponent knew exactly what to expect from the other, and nothing seems to give them a new advantage. The element of surprise is gone, and strategy is exhausted. One waits to win like an old man waits to die – something will happen regardless. It is bound to happen. Isner v. Mahut lasted eleven hours and five minutes, over three days, and is to date the longest tennis game ever played.

The bout in bouldering has many stages, and one of those is indeed the fight when the sequence has been hammered out, and one is left only with attempts and execution. These are the late stages of the project. But there is another bout in bouldering, and it is envisioning the line in the first place. It is hard to say exactly where inspiration comes from or know when a line is possible or how we come to commit to a problem. This vision to see a line marks the highest calibre of a boulderer. This is why so much weight is put onto the athlete who develops new lines, who, in essence, establishes new performances, for only they can be called an *avant-garde* athlete. They have seen *marks* where others did not, or they have had the determination and resolve to commit time and labour to something that might, in the end, not work out. And things often do not work out, but that just makes the ones that do all the sweeter.

> There are things known and there are things unknown, and in between are the doors of perception.
>
> Aldous Huxley

No bout is more famous than the Bachar–Kauk battle, beginning in 1978, over the first ascent of *Midnight Lightning*. Said to have been imagined by a 'hallucinating' John Yablonski, the line that is now *Midnight Lightning*, in Camp 4's Yosemite, was once a dream in the technical sense of the word. Its movement was only imaginary, as it had not yet been realised in a body.

In the storied history of the first ascent of 'Midnight', we can perhaps find a gem of understanding; first in the fact that Yablonski was said to 'hallucinate', and second, how this hallucination was written into bouldering history. Here was the altered state of reality needed for a mind to see something others cannot see – a clean 'door of perception', to borrow a phrase from Aldous Huxley, from which Jim Morrison's band *The Doors* got their name. But we have here got into the realm of psychedelia and the mystical vision of saints and madmen, close cousins of the fantastic. Which could not be more apt, for the problem was said to have been 'seen' by Yablonski while on acid and was named after a Jimmy Hendrix song.

If it is a performance that is achieved each time a new line is opened, the creative process is not akin to that of other performative arts. For one, we have to imagine a solution alongside the brute resistance of the stone, where some solutions just are not possible. We have to release the cliché of stock movement we have in our minds to allow a new sequence to enter, and we must also show faith in the process that our dedication will pay dividends. In this manner, the problem opens to us, with 'us' as the passive recipient of an 'outside' force entering our consciousness. Yet, this is also another way of saying that the ultimate source of 'knowing' a line 'will go' comes from a place that cannot be pinned down – it remains *apophatic* (unable to be spoken of). Like midnight lightning that strikes at the darkest hour, illuminating the sky with blinding vision, so too does possible movement strike into consciousness. Just as quickly as movement is mysteriously lost to the boulderer – 'I just can't feel that anymore' – it is mysteriously discovered. This dialectic between being in the know and being in the dark is precisely the slippage that challenges all athletics, for if sports are anything outside joyful acts, they are jabs at mastering the unconquerable: the foot with a ball, the arm with a pitch, the swing with a club, the floor with the tumble. This tells us less about sports and more about what we are trying to do when living in a body. And second, what we are trying to do is worth repeating. I've laid in bed countless nights thinking about a project only for an idea to pop out of nowhere to try a different foot on that crux move, which of course, I do the next time and send. The more we can listen to these cues from our unconscious, the better.

Often, the storied folklore of a boulder problem gets us excited about it, perhaps the idea that it is temperamental, stubborn, finicky; we too want to take part in the Greek idea of *agon* – the contest. But what was the fight really about?

Did it have any victories? What or who was being fought? What is really accomplished when the fight is over?

If one were to follow the strain that the body undergoes when bouldering, it would be like blotches of intensity glowing red hot across specific parts of the limbs, only to have such zones shift slowly to other areas like a flame across a dry field. Thanks to Gilles Deleuze, we can call this process a *de-territorialisation*. The rock forces us to re-territorialise the stored energies in our body. The back right shoulder glows while the right foot turns cold as it cuts. A right heel hook moves the energy to the hamstring, and while the sum of energy is neither gained nor lost, as in the second law of thermodynamics, the bouldering body needs to make a habit of efficient *shiftings* of energy. We usually call it balance, but this is too imprecise a term to describe the body's violent energies.

What is a constant in a boulder problem is one's weight. For instance, I weigh 168lb (76kg) at all times during a send. My body will never shed this weight. When we think we take weight in certain moves, such as the heel hook on the UK's *Brad Pitt*, we just transfer that weight to other parts of the body in contact with the stone, which now must navigate movement with that transferred weight. Of course, a table takes the weight of a person when we sit on it. Yet, when we do so, the table must 'think' differently, and even then, thinking is misleading since the boulderer need not so much think as develop an instantaneous feedback loop between their body and mind. We could say with a fair amount of correctness that on *Brad Pitt* the rock takes on the weight of the left foot, and we would be correct to think so. However, we are taking the notion of weight too abstractly. Standing still, we have weight. A silent rock on a hillside has a weight. A body in motion does not weight in this manner – weight shifts and travels. Stand up straight and lift a leg, and you'll fall over. Managing weight comes with movement. A heel hook does allow the body to take weight, but in the same manner, it merely forces us to use our weight differently. Right before our eyes, the absence of weight morphs into an increased complexity of movement. Assuming the most fundamental stance – standing still – every movement is an alteration of weight, shifting from simplicity to complexity. It's a compromise: we trade simplicity for efficiency or, in the rules of the game, effectiveness. What is effective is rarely the simplest move, but this is the game we play.

In preparing for a dyno, for a split second, my back shoulders are loaded with twice my body weight or more, busy as they are preparing to compensate for full gravity while I'm in the air. Because my body exerts no energy when in the air, it must exert all its energy on the front end, and it will feel this vacation of energy on the back end as well when the body latches the hold and extends itself, and the weight returns full force to my fingers. Hence, dynoing to small holds is really hard – the body must exert the exact amount of force to cover for all this, and the successful dyno is precisely the result of this equation. The impact is felt on both sides of weightlessness, in the release *and* in the catch. The revolution from climbing to bouldering can be read through this hermeneutic of dynamic movement, and specifically through bouldering.

When in a dyno, a vital energy is released, serving to open the door to an entirely different genre of movement. Surfing experienced such a revolution when its athletes performed tricks in the air, *above* the wave. Skateboarding had a similar revolution, and *Dogtown and Z-Boys* (2001) spoke of the moment when California skateboarders extended their axles *above* the concrete coping of a pool. For the skateboarders, the day was sunny, and the psyche was high, and the pressure was building for the move. And then it happened, captured in a classic photo of the lift-off moment: the primal scene of modern skateboarding

– aerial moves, pure freedom, absolute flotation, a space in which the rules of gravity worked only in the abstract; that is, they were to be felt solely on the landing. The skater had long hair, was shirtless, I think and encapsulated an era. This was counter-culture, the revolutionary act of youth – an act, we must remember, characteristic of the 60s and 70s: rebellion against the 1950's generation, jobs, careerism, 2.5 kids, Cadillac. But it had happened – the board and the person rose above the constricting frame of the pool. Skateboarding would no longer be tied to the movements of surfing and fluid lines on the pavement, to which it owes its lineage, but could now branch off into undiscovered territory. Something about the move stored in this *passage* opened itself up to new genres of being and affects for a skateboarder.

Contemporary surfers are no longer tied to the wave, as they had been historically, and now borrow tricks from snowboarding (540 grabs) and skateboarding (the kick-flip). Surfing exited the wave and entered the air around the late 1970s, though airs did occur in the 1960s. Regardless of the precise date, this type of movement was a revolution in the sport. It brought a newfound sense of freedom to its practitioners, embodied in that split second of being airborne and the potential that this moment provided. Likewise, the release move in gymnastics opened up an entirely new range of skills, and one cannot be a successful gymnast today without being able to execute a wide range of release moves, which, if one looks into gymnastics' history, are far from common at the outset, especially on the bar events.

Skateboarding and bouldering share an aesthetic fascination: *the line*. The line, for skaters, is the sequence of tricks done together without falling or messing up. It is usually a sequence of tricks linked together across, say, a park – *360 flip* here, *k-grind* there, *frontside flip* here, *switch-heel* over the final ten stairs. Watch a skate video, and you'll see tons of them. For a good line, what matters is not each trick, but the sequence of tricks strung together. Some skaters are known for famous lines, and often the best lines can never be repeated. One is always unsure how the line will go, and often if you are feeling lucky, you just keep going and landing the tricks. Like a boulder problem, a sequence of moves is strung together as a line – a boulder problem is rarely one move. Like the gymnastic routine, the problem is the *linking* of the sequence.

Many would think that it gets more difficult to complete a hard boulder problem because of what is taken away when trying to send (focus, strength, to name but two). But it is the opposite – it is what is added that makes a line so difficult: the pressure to succeed now that one had descended further into that strange realm called success; the more success one has, the bigger the pressure. Anxiety builds. The heart quickens on the final topout . . . and then, on that easy exit move, you botch it, despite having done it dozens of times, easily. Of course, 'psyche' is a powerful motivation and often takes credit for the send. Yet, in a poll of high-end athletes, nearly all say that they are in the groove about 20 per cent of the time, which leaves a large chunk for just hanging on when things aren't going well.

The line is the skater's style. Some skaters stay on the flats, like Daewon Song or Rodney Mullen; others hit the stairs, like Jeremy Wray or Jamie Thomas. The line is the expression of the skater and the types of moves they prefer individually. One does not ask if a line in skateboarding is contrived. Contrivance *is* expression.

⌘

LIPS AND FINGERS

The shock of latching a good dyno is like a minor death strung out over a few seconds. The pull-shock the muscles and tendons receive when latching a hold is the contrary of a push-shock sensation, as one might experience when jumping up and hitting the ceiling with your body stiff and taut. The impact is the same for the body. Yet, the extension of movement, in the form of the body's stretching in the dyno, overcomes the movement's internal violence, the muscle tears, or the hand's death grip. The body elongates, then, in a split second, recoils. The muscles need to tense to gain their strength. It's odd, but the body's pain is traded for the joy it receives, and the tearing of muscle is shrouded in the pure experience of movement. For instance, a hard dyno is not unlike a hard squat or bench press you do at the gym. Still, a *je ne sais quoi* in the body's dynamic motion shrouds the crude exertion factor, putting aesthetic-athletic experience firmly in its place. We might say it's 'such a good problem', and of course, we mean it is aesthetic (not choss, and that it is a good line with quality holds), but the problem would be nothing without *quality* movement. A classic problem is like a good baseball stadium or an itinerant 'home field': a process of natural selection has granted this problem credibility and iconic status. Quality movement results from our body's kinesiology (a tweaky shouldery move is rarely quality) when combined with holds that feel good, sequences that are pleasing for some reason, among others.

According to the gate-control theory, developed by Melzack & Wall (1965), pleasure has the potential to block out pain. A neural mechanism in the spinal cord can act as a gate, essentially filtering out which nerve impulses go to the brain. Pain is usually classified into two areas: acute and chronic. Acute pain is the result of a trauma, such as a torn A3 pulley, while chronic is your forearm tendonitis. Boulderers no doubt suffer from acute pain, though one could say that chronic pain is the result of too much acute pain, over and over, until it eventually affects the proper functioning of the body.

Certain control techniques utilising the gate-control theory have applied some of the theory's discoveries to chronic pain sufferers. They have discovered that purposeful activity is one of the best ways to condition the gate to allow some impulses and deny others. In essence, the joy we receive from movement blocks out all potential pain done to our body. The body's natural mechanism for avoiding injury in acute situations, the reflex mechanism, is often overridden by the desire to remain in motion and also, of course, the desire to top out your project.

The body parts that contain the most nerve endings are the lips and the fingertips, and so, by extension, our hands *taste* the world. The body part with the fewest nerve endings is the middle of the back. In climbing of all types, the body becomes a hand, speaks through it, feels through it, gains its confidence through the hand's confidence. The flood sensation from the fingertips masks the rest of the violence done to our body. We partake in a sport of touch. But sensation is knowledge as well. Grab a loose flake on the top of a highball, and one immediately feels the entire body freeze. Non-linguistic data is communicated instantaneously to your brain. Your body responds immediately, almost always bypassing cognitive and reflective thought. You pull on that flake less, adjust your feet, ensure that your other hand can hold if the flake pulls. You look down, contemplating your fate.

There is also substantial scientific evidence linking zones of increased nerve sensitivity to fantasy (one should get my drift here). One could conclude rather unscientifically that the accepted notion that climbers often fantasise about grabbing the holds on their projects is because our skin, at least the zones with a lot of nerve endings, just happen to be built like that organ used for sexual pleasure.

But there is an irony here. Our skin becomes calloused with repeated use, making our fingertips less sensitive, a problem, of course, we remedy by sanding our tips. Yet, at the same time, this extreme sensitivity, once the property of our skin, becomes the property of our entire body. Our fingertips do not shred from sitting still but become worn down when the body moves under them unnaturally. Subtle or not-so-subtle shiftings of weight tear or wear down our skin over time. What skin responds to is the pain of bouldering movement, and calloused skin allows our entire body to move as it wishes without causing pain; like muscle fibres adapting after stress, skin does the same. Calloused skin protects us, allowing what was once a sensitivity in a particular area (the fingertip) to dissolve, as it were, across the entirety of the body.

⌘

A GENERATIVE MACHINE

The dance, just as the performance of the actor, is kinaesthetic art, art of the muscle sense. The awareness of tension and relaxation within his own body, the sense of balance that distinguishes the proud stability of the vertical from the risky adventures of thrusting and falling – these are the tools of the dancer.

Rudolf Arnheim

It is well known in acting theory that one can generate certain emotions by moving your body in a certain way or putting the body into the gesture that accompanies the emotion. If an actor is having trouble feeling anger, they do what an angry person does, and anger follows. Trouble feeling sad? Slump down, look at the floor, move your limbs slowly and with the least amount of energy. Sadness will soon descend on you; it arrives like an alien but unwanted friend. It will soon feel at home, and your body won't reject it because it was your body that brought it. The body is a generative machine, flooding its surface with affects (powers to move the body), constantly producing this or that force. Sitting has a mood as powerful as sprinting. Researchers say that putting your lips and face into the position of a smile can make you feel happier.

Emotions are usually understood in abstract, conceptual terms – sadness, anger, anxiety, joy, pride. This is the language of unfortunate simplicity. Language always simplifies. But before they are given recognisable coordinates in the form of concepts, emotions are raucous, wild, and unbundled. Emotions are small ecosystems of the body without essence or orderly constitution, and they cross borders all the time, making their understanding impossible even for the most trained bodhisattva. For instance, you get an ego boost from sending your project, but in reality it has little to do with linking six hard moves, but rather your girlfriend left you, and you got fired from your job, and this boulder problem was all you had, and so you leaned on it for your happiness. Emotions are topographical spaces through which we name the body's most profound and complex processes. A name like 'joy' does not define the process, and as Freud said of pleasure, it is a 'discharge' that attempts to return the body to an earlier state of equilibrium. Joy is not an addition. Joy is then essential to the proper working of the body and not a decadent addition to a boring life. Something authentic in the body desires the discharge that joy produces.

Emotions are electric charges in the body *before* they are concepts. Thinking you know an emotion from its name is like saying you know a mountain because you know information about it. Emotions can be classified by quality (earned or unearned, superficial, or authentic, destructive or constructive) and intensity (strong or weak, short or long duration, wild or tame). Each emotion is specific to a time and place – it is a singularity. By understanding the subterranean forces (the affects) that condition the emotion-concept, we can then assign sports a place in the body's general matrix. More than just being specific to time and place affects are products of specific postures, localities, and mind/brain habit patterns. As the body makes its way through a boulder problem, we may not immediately be aware of the affects emitted by our postures, yet they *are* there, as present as sounds our ears cannot hear. Whether or not it is conscious or not, the conditions informing our emotions are just that – actively influential.

We see a small fraction of the light spectrum, about a thousandth of one per cent, yet the spectrum is there, omnipresent. Technologies allow us to 'see' the rest. This brings up an interesting point – does bouldering take part in a silencing of the body's radical affects? Or is there, within the endorphin-rushed movement, a cloak that mutes the body's spastic energies in such a way that it renders us incapable of feeling what bouldering does to us?

Perhaps the best climbers can recycle the mass of disorganised and untamed affects produced by the body's multiple postures into calm, effective energy. Given their smooth style, Jimmy Webb and Dai Koyamada strike me as prime examples. This is much more than poise amidst difficulty. On the opposite spectrum lies the beginner who cannot control their body as they pass through a difficult sequence; it is not that the body is unruly for them, for they can walk and do other activities just fine – it is rather that movement has caught them off guard and they cannot control it fast enough. For example, to hold a handstand, you need to know the precise point where weight shifts, and you need to react immediately on a micro-level (it's all in the fingers and wrists), whereas a beginner will have to walk their hands to regain equilibrium. A veteran climber will have developed the requisite muscular control to move in control, and these fibres take years to develop. A good and experienced boulderer navigates movement with similar dexterity. A unique bouldering term like 're-adjust', for example, only highlights how the difference between success and failure in our sport can often be a matter of how the hold feels beneath our fingertips. If it feels bad on our fingertips, our body will react accordingly and lose confidence, which negatively affects success.

What is sport? What is it then that men put into sport? Themselves, their human universe. Sport is made in order to speak the human contract . . . Ultimately man knows certain forces, certain conflicts, joys and agonies; sport expresses them, liberates them, consumes them without ever letting anything be destroyed.

Roland Barthes

Bouldering exists because it exploits an untapped joy that has no precedent in history. Sports exist and can be defined by the emotions they impart to athletes, as each sport is a virtual catalogue of the body's potential for movements. Only in sports are certain feelings felt and emotions expressed, and this because the body is put in situations it otherwise doesn't experience in daily life (habitual movement). Boulder problems have their own joys, and no two problems are alike in terms of the joy they produce because each one singularly organises the body – the posture is a window into an experience.

Runners have runner's high, surfers have their stoke, soccer players their zone, dancers their plasticity, climbers their lightness. It can only be felt internally, but it is immediately a trait of muscle, and that feeling is an attribute of John Gill's 'bodily state of affairs'. Boulderers are ceaselessly bombarded with psyche after completing a problem. We top out drunk in sensation; our bodies flushed with the most beautiful sensations the body can produce. We are addicted to certain moves, and the joy a problem produces often makes or breaks the reputation of that problem. The subtle body position that one must employ to static Gill's *Pinch Overhang* in Horsetooth Reservoir, Colorado, feels so right that I do it only to feel *that* move. My body craves this move, and it puts me in front of the boulder every time as a dog to a hunk of meat. After a ten-year hiatus from that problem, I returned and did that move, and it felt exactly as I had remembered, like visiting an old friend.

It is only natural that yoga is allied to bouldering and climbing. Aside from common business interests – a similar demographic – it shares with bouldering a practice of executing postures, inhabiting specific configurations and maintaining balance under duress. And, aside from 'achievement' (which does not technically belong to yoga, it being more the practice of inhabiting a pose more fully than it is about *doing* a pose), yoga is a therapeutic activity designed to have lasting effects in one's life as well as in one's physical body. Sports thrive because of what they provide for those who practise them. If a sport does not bring joy to its practitioners, it is finished, and a new sport will take its place. Sensibilities change throughout history, and what was satisfying to a 15th century Frenchman may not appetize a modern-day athlete, but this does not mean that what a sport generates in the body does change. Sprinting 100 meters circa 400 BCE generated the same affects in the body as sprinting 100 meters today, though the emotional interpretation may differ.

For instance, just glance through B. K. S. Iyengar's *Light on Yoga* and one will find specific postures with descriptions of technique and effects. One posture, called *Salamba Sarvangasana I* (shoulder-stand), is executed when one lays on the back, raises the legs and hips vertically while being supported by the top of the spine; the arms keep the balance, and one's palms push into the back, which keeps the body from falling. The move is *ceremonialised* and broken down into many steps. Each step requires consciousness in breath. As for the effects, Iyengar writes that 'the importance of *Sarvangasana* cannot be overemphasised. It is one of the greatest boons conferred on humanity by our ancient sages.' Iyengar speaks of the beneficial effects on the glands of this exercise, how blood flows to the heart with the effortless help of gravity, how it can help asthma, bronchitis and throat ailments. Continued practise of this move can ease nervous breakdowns, insomnia, menstrual troubles – and the list goes on. Iyengar finishes this small section: 'It is no overstatement to say that if a person regularly practises *Sarvangasana* he will feel new vigour and strength and will be happy and confident. New life will flow into him, his mind will be at peace and he will feel the joy of life.'

One would be tempted to call such an analysis ridiculous and argue that we attribute these moves to these powers because of the religions of the people describing and practising them. One would be correct were it not for the thousands of years that Indian practitioners have devoted to yogic postures and their effects on the body, incorporated in various forms of 'legitimate' and effective medicine. The same goes for manipulation of the body's Chi energy in Chinese medicinal practice: a type of medicine that is only now just beginning to be covered by US insurance companies, perhaps spearheaded by reports of Iraqi and Afghan veterans who swear that acupuncture is doing more to help their injuries than Western medicine.

What yoga, and philosophy for that matter, can do is bring a microscope onto the subtle tremors the body undergoes in these postures. Is yogic practice an unconscious 'voice' of bodily movement akin to the element in the chemical compound? Do we find in its unparalleled analysis the types of things happening in the body in other, more complex movements? There is no doubt that for the types of moves boulderers do, the actual beneficial effects of the movements – emotional, therapeutic, physical, etc. – are clouded in their complexity. Mix ten colours, and you'll end up with brown. Trying to discern after the fact, staring at a brown paste, what colours went into that mix is impossible. The specific contribution singular moves make to the overall emotion become mixed in the final sensation. Still, we must remember, it is only due to *specificity* that we have the *general*.

Certain moves may produce this, in the same manner as yoga, but by the time we top out, they have all entered a pot and been so mixed together that one could never decipher them individually; not to mention the fact that the dynamic moves we perform make a type of yogic observation next to impossible. Could one do this type of analysis in isolation, on a tricky cross-through, say? Without question, we are doing the moves as dance and yoga – gathering, contracting, repulsing, expanding – except just by another name. What our bodies are undergoing will forever lie below the threshold of consciousness, perhaps the better for it, but the fact that we are reaping psychosomatic benefits from movement itself is undeniable. Athletics, in general, share and promote these benefits: joy, wellbeing, vitality. This is why athletics exists as a societal phenomenon.

Because they provide joy, athletics must be acting against some form of pain, whether this pain is personal or existential (caused by the alienation of modern life in general). The relation between boulderer and their art of touch seeks to alleviate the body from what it is not doing when it boulders, such as standing or walking (habit). In what is perhaps the best book on pain written to date, Elaine Scarry makes the following observations about human invention: 'The human body, troubled by weight, creates a chair; the chair recreates him to be weightless.' One could say the same thing about bouldering: the human body, troubled by pain, creates a boulder problem; the boulder problem creates joy in place of pain.

Before you begin training in enlightenment, a bowl is a bowl and tea is tea. During training, a bowl is not a bowl, and tea is not tea. After enlightenment, a bowl is a bowl and tea is tea.

Zen proverb

Hai Wo is a master of the Japanese tea ceremony. It is said that he was the best. To have tea served by him is to have tea made directly from the heart, and to be in the presence of a pure heart is a rare occasion. Like any tea master, he spends all day with the details of the ceremony: he thinks about who is coming, where they will sit and how to adjust his setting and gestures to them specifically, for the ceremony is as much about the guests as it is anything. Wo purifies his hands before the guests arrive, and throughout the night his every move is catered perfectly to their presence – he sets the table according to their line of vision, walks a certain way, and bends in a certain way. And the night goes perfectly; his movements and hospitality are so in tune as to be both completely visible and yet invisible. His guests feel honoured and believe they have witnessed a one-of-a-kind experience.

But Wo is known more for another skill – the lifting of his left hand. Sure, anyone can do it, but it is well known in this part of central Japan that when Wo raises his hand, it is different; something about it encapsulates the Japanese value of intentional, thoughtful movements. Wo is a master of such movements. Like the Shaolin monks of China who retreat into solitude for decades to find and master centuries-forgotten skills, Wo does not so much practise this move as allow this move to come freely from his body. Experts in the trade consider Wo's trick just as impressive as Hai Tank's one-finger handstand trick, though to the untrained eye, Wo's trick is much 'easier'. True, it did require a lot of training and skill at one time, but now, it is so engrained in Wo's body that he can focus on different aspects of the movement.

He is called to give lectures to schools, and it is said that at the end of his talks, he will perform his hand raise, and even schoolchildren will sit in awe. He will stand there, a smile washing across his face. He will breathe in and out a few times, then, as he breathes outwards, his arm begins to rise slowly, almost automatically, as if it were not his hand, not his intention to move it, as if it were just moving of its own accord, and so smoothly that one would never think it was bone and muscle under his skin but rather cotton or silk; it rises to a vertical position, then descends as he exhales; his body inhabits his arm so profoundly for those few seconds that he feels completely rejuvenated afterwards.

To speak of the quality of movement as 'easy' or 'hard', or better or worse, is completely to miss the point.

French painter Paul Cezanne's apple is not a better-painted apple than others, for that would make his painting obsolete in the face of photography. What Cezanne did was capture what an apple is *about*. He inhabited an apple with more precision and sensitivity than others. Astonishingly, it is said that Cezanne required 100 working sessions for a still life, which can amount to over 500 hours of 'looking' just to paint an apple. But what apples! Cezanne could have chosen to master the twisting body in the throes of battle, as Michelangelo would have, and so prove to the world that he was the best painter, but he didn't. He chose an apple, and we can only assume that the act of looking was more pleasing to Cezanne than finishing a painting.

Like Cezanne, Hai Wo is not concerned with the difficulty of movement, or doing it better than others, or creating something monumental. Perhaps it is something much more tangible that motivates him. Something much more mysterious because it is tangible. Perhaps for a fleeting second, to boulder is to feel what a body can do, *what it is*, and what it is to inhabit, brutally and naively, the joy of movement itself.

⌘

FURTHER READING

Pat Ament, *John Gill: Master of Rock* (Stackpole Books, 1998)

John Gill, 'The Art of Bouldering' (The American Alpine Club Journal, 1969)

Wolfgang Güllich, 'Atmosphere and Lifestyle', in *A Life in the Vertical* (Menasha Ridge Press Inc., 1995)

Tara Magdalinski, *Sport, Technology and the Body: The Nature of Performance* (Routledge, 2009)

Neil Lewis, 'The Climbing Body, Nature and the Experience of Modernity', in *Bodies of Nature* (Sage Publications, 2001)

Dale Goddard and Udo Neumann, *Performance Rock Climbing* (Stackpole Books, 1993)

Susan Foster, *Taken by Surprise: A Dance Improvisation Reader* (Wesleyan, 2003)

Bruce Lee, *Tao of Jeet Kune Do* (Black Belt Communications, 1995)

John Sherman, *Stone Crusade* (The American Alpine Club, 1994)

John Sherman, *Better Bouldering* (Falcon Guides, 1997)

PHOTOGRAPHY

Frontispiece
Greg Kerzhner climbing in Rocklands, South Africa © Tara Kerzhner

Page 6
John Gill on *Left Eliminator*, Fort Collins, 1968 © John Gill

Page 13
The author on *The Pinch Overhang* © John Sherman

Page 23
Udo Neumann in mid dyno © Udo Neumann

Page 32
Michaela Kiersch on *Jedi Mind Tricks* (V4) in the early morning
light, Bishop, California. © Christopher Beauchamp

Page 49
Michaela Kiersch on *Saigon Direct* (V8), Bishop
California © Christopher Beauchamp

Page 68
Charlotte Bosley on Hueco's *Speed Bump* © Dan Brayack

Page 78
Jason Kehl on *Beer Aktion* © Ally Dorey

Page 89
Michaela Kirsch on the Druid Stone's *Kojakian Wisdom
Reworked*, Bishop © Christopher Beauchamp

Page 95
Pawtuckaway, New Hampshire © Christopher Beauchamp

Page 107
The mega-classic *Mandala* (V12), Bishop, California © Boone Speed

Page 135
Bouldering at Bishop © Christopher Beauchamp